BureaucraZy

The Razor's Edge

Attention Authors

'We Convert Fighters into Writers'. That has been the motto of Manas Publications, since more than four decades. Our message to the world is that India can win the battle, not only by the bullet but also by the pen. There is no dearth of intellectuals in our country, but their knowledge is confined to them only. No sincere effort has been made by any other publisher to channelise their knowledge in national interest. That is why the talent of a large number of intellectuals, remains latent. An author transforms his knowledge, into a manuscript, and it is our job to spread his/her knowledge by converting it into a beautiful book.

For over four decades, Manas has been motivating the intellectuals by publishing their manuscripts and would like to publish your manuscript too. If you or your colleagues have any manuscript, ready for publication or are working on it, kindly contact us with detailed synopsis and the list of contents. We would transform your work, into a valuable publication. If you wish, we can also suggest you, the suitable subjects for writing books, related to your area of expertise. Manas is known for its publishing quality and commitments. We take utmost care in production and give wide publicity to the book, as well as its author, through our national and international distribution network.

BureaucraZy
The Razor's Edge

Amulya Ratna Nanda

IAS (Retired)

Former Secretary to Government of India

Manas Publications

(We Convert Fighters into Writers)

New Delhi-110002 (INDIA)

MANAS PUBLICATIONS
(We convert Fighters into Writers)
(Publishers, Distributors, Importers & Exporters)
4402/5-A, Ansari Road (Opp. HDFC Bank)
Darya Ganj, New Delhi-110 002 (India)
Off. 23260783, 23265523, Res. 23842660
Fax: 011-23272766
E-mail: manaspublications@gmail.com
manaspublications@yahoo.com
Website: www.manaspublications.in

ISBN 978-81-7049-515-4
₹ 695/-

Designed at Innovative Processors
Printed in India at
R.K. Print Services, Delhi and
Published by Mrs Suman Lata for
Manas Publications, 4402/5-A, Ansari Road (Opp. HDFC Bank),
Darya Ganj, New Delhi-110 002 (INDIA)

Dedicated to the

Memory of my parents, two elder sisters
and wife, Manorama, who are no more

Contents

Acknowledgement

Writing an autobiographical memoir was not in my thoughts, until 2011, when my three daughters, Bizee, Lizee and Lita broached the idea. Some friends from the civil society working closely with me also prodded me on this initiative. Somehow, I started writing as I came into nostalgic frame of mind sometime in 2011 and completed in 2015. I must acknowledge the encourgement I received from my daughters and grand daughters in this venture.

I have shared the first draft with some intimate friends (B.B. Lal, P.K. Das and K.G. Verma all batchmates in IAS) and received suggestions and comments. The inspirational advice given by my friend, philosopher and guide, Dr. C.B. Satpathy was very helpful in shaping the final draft. I am grateful to all of them.

I acknowledge the initiative taken by Manas Publications for publication of the book.

Last but not the least, I must express my sincere gratitude to Akritti Bhatia, who helped me in computer typing of my handwritten manuscript.

Prologue

Many ICS and IAS officers have written their memoirs or autobiographies. There is not much new or unique in describing the chronicles of an administrative officer. Experiences vary to a degree from one to the other; perceptions and feelings differ; but stating the gross facts is not very interesting, except perhaps to readers from the same tribe.

I am trying to share the quintessence of my life's experiences so far, with my perception and memory of the gross facts, as well as of the subtle aspects in an as unbiased a manner as possible. It is not my intention to justify all my actions or to denigrate some people maliciously. I do not wish to blow my own trumpets in an ego trip and get a sense of satisfaction of self-righteousness.

The gross journey of life for everyone follows a more or less uniform growth pattern from childhood to adolescence to youth to middle age to the elderly stage (young old to old old), unless some end the journey mid-way. There is a subtle journey of the mental, emotional and spiritual world within which it moves in its own stride, in each case depending on many factors – inborn, circumstantial, or of one's own making in the complex interplay of the three 'gunas' of Prakriti- Sattwa, Rajas and Tamas.

As I relate the events, relationships and happenings of my gross life's memoirs, I reflect on the subtle thoughts and perceptions at every stage. I try to present the facts and characters as per my subtle perceptions, which may or may not be agreeable or palatable to some people, who may have a completely different or contradictory view of the same. With malice towards none, I present the gross and subtle threads of memories of the past in as fair and accurate a manner as possible with my limited wisdom. I do not intend to hurt anyone's sentiments. I beg to be pardoned for any omissions or commissions of frailties or misconceptions from my side.

The Memoirs are divided into two parts. ***Part - I*** captioned 'Life's Gross Journey' captures the story of birth, parentage, sibling relationships, childhood, education, marriage, family and the working career in teaching (1964) civil service (1964-2002) and the civil society activism (2002- 2015). A part of this story is more personal – joys and sorrows, comedies and tragedies, glamour, humour and the play of destiny. Some aspects of human relationships have societal overtones. I have tried to be as frank and true to myself and society as possible.

As I write my gross life's memoirs, my mind is enveloped by the emotive ghazal of Nissar Akhtar, *'The Last Meeting'*. To quote Nissar: Excerpts from *'The Last Meeting'*:

"Some relationships almost over
Some friends all forgotten
Some pictures badly drawn
Some write-ups dim and hazy
Some tears ready to burst
Some pearls fallen on the cheek
Some signs, all astonished
Some images, all afloat
Some world almost desolate
Some dreams nearly shattered –
They are all my own, they are no strangers;
Stop them not, let them come
They have come to meet me;
They are such shadowy figures
That I may not even recognise them, though ...."

(*The Last Meeting*, Jaan Nissar Akhtar, translated by Kuldip Salil)

The major part of the story in Part - I deals with my journey through the long working career in Civil Service in the Government, starting with one year of Indian Revenue Service (Income Tax) and thereafter for 37 years in the Indian Administrative Service. I spent 15 years working on the Government of India assignments, and the rest in the state government of Odisha. I have tried to present some interesting aspects of work in each assignment along with the trials and tribulations faced in the course of working. Policy, laws and programme implementation, oversight and formulation in 'public interest' have been the sum total of the job assignments in the middle and senior levels of bureaucracy. It has been generally a "generalist" leadership management career, with an overdose of expertise or specialisation in some areas of work. By strange coincidence, my postings in 'Census', 'Health, Population and Development' were preceded by an intensive mid-career academic study on 'Population' abroad. My entrenchment in census and population study brought me some recognition from the world of demographers and public health to be considered as some sort of a specialist among the generalists' in the IAS and beyond in the Civil Society activism and institution- building in which I have been associated for over a decade after my superannuation from Government Service.

I have tried to analyse important issues I was confronted with at each stage of the Government Service – from Sub-division to District to Division to the State Government and Central Government Ministries and offices. Apart from inter-personal, human and financial resources issues in administration, there were broader issues of society and societal development. I have attempted to present such issues of public interest, along with the complex web of political-bureaucratic-civil society interests, amidst which I played my role (along with my colleagues) to tackle the issues at hand. In the face of confrontation at times, I stuck to the principles of 'public interest', 'ethics' and 'non- discrimination' (positive discrimination, wherever required), raised my head high and remained unscathed and unruffled by and large in the midst of threats and temptations. This I feel as a blessing of God and the help of an invisible hand of my Sadguru (Perfect Master of Spirituality) all through.

I have a tryst with two types of serious conflicts the country witnessed in the 1960s and 1970s – the first wave of the Naxalite movement gathering steam in the late 60s and early 70s in the tribal belt and surrounding areas in Odisha and Andhra Pradesh. The brand of Naxalite movement originating in Naxalbari in West Bengal under the leadership of Charu Mazumdar and Kanhu Sanyal was taking roots in the inaccessible tribal belt of Srikakulam district in Andhra and Parlakhemundi sub-division of Ganjam district (where I worked as the Sub-collector) and Rayayada-Guupur areas of Koraput district in Odisha. The young educated groups of doctors, lawyers, teachers and leftist intellectuals were providing fodder of ideas to penetrate into the minds of the poor and downtrodden including tribals, who were exploited by traders, money lenders and land grabbers. What was witnessed in the 1960s and 70s have now (over next 40 years) solidified with intensity and spread to the vast expanse of a belt with corridors over Andhra, Odisha, Chhattisgarh, Jharkhand, Bihar, Maharashtra and beyond. The initial idealism has gradually become a ruse to extract money and weaponry from many sources, posing grave threat to the nation. Strategies toward it, which worked fairly well earlier, do not seem to be working now.

The second national crisis I witnessed as an active district officer was the Emergency of 1975-76. I have not reconciled to the rationale or justification for the imposition of a nation-wide emergency, as my experience will be related in Part - I. I did not allow excesses in my district despite pressures and temptation of exercising power and authority.

Two other significant developments over the forty years of my working career have been the socio-demographic transition and the economic policy changes, starting in the 1980s, but more resolutely in the 1990s and beyond. There have been positive and negative fall-outs of both these transitions, which were inter-related in many aspects. There were global developments impinging in many ways on India. As I got associated with some aspects of these socio- economic-demographic transitions in the 1970s, 80s and 90s in the arena of policy strategisation or implementation, I had some inkling of the challenges, contestations and inner contradictions of the process of change, particularly from the interest angle of the poor, women and marginalised in India. Even the policy prescriptions have been ad hoc and of knee-jerk response and sometimes counterproductive.

As I will narrate my memoirs in Part - I, I will present the perception on various policy decisions of the Government in the areas of my work and their implications.

Part - II captioned 'Mystic Journey' unravels my spiritual journey into the world of mysticism. It may appear as an esoteric fad fit to be dismissed as a very personal belief or faith not amenable to reason, but it provides mental and emotional comfort at an advanced age.

From the 1990s, I have been struck by the Shirdi Sai phenomenon, and I am trying to look 'within' to re-discover Truth. As I relate the chronicles of my childhood, adolescence, youth, adult life and life as an elderly, I try to give meaning to every event, occurrence or experience I remember. I discover the Karmik philosophy of 'Deha Prarabdha' and 'Karma Phal' (Destiny) in these occurrences or experiences affecting me. I see clearly the interplay of the tendencies and proclivities of Tamas, Rajas and Sattva. I see the hidden hand of protection of a higher power saving me from emotional morass and moral downfall. I am aware of the play of destiny and the need for patience, perseverance and fortitude (SABURI) at all stages. My Perfect Master (Sadguru), Shirdi Sai Baba has come in my life, and with His Grace, I am able to weave a pattern to this life. Ego and pride of the service career slowly gave way to a more balanced Self, which is more in tune with the laws of Nature. As I look back, I feel that life would have been much better, had I come to Sai's Feet earlier.

The transition in a Sai devotee like me has been very slow, but steady. The impressions of so many past lives and even of this life are difficult to erase. Many hurdles come in the way. Walking on the path of Devotion is like treading on a razor's edge. A very cautious and conscientious approach is required at every stage on issues of life and death, joys and sorrows, human relationships and time utilization.

As I crossed the seventy years of my present gross life, I reflect with awe and wonder ('Visamad' as Guru Nanak used to say) the Grace of the Almighty God – the Absolute Truth, and my Sadguru, Shirdi Sai Baba. I am now a septuagenarian by gross experience, but a child at heart trying to perceive subtle spiritual truths. I feel the 'child' within me in my spiritual life, nursing no ego in what I have achieved. It is all God given through my Sadguru's Grace.

The name, fame, power or social recognition earned during my days in the IAS career pale into insignificance before this new dawn of life's experience on the SAI path. Of course, I do not intend to denigrate the earlier experiences. I enjoyed every bit of it then, and as I look at it in retrospect, I derive a sense of contentment, as God given. I repent for the follies and mistakes I committed, and pray to Sai to give me the strength and opportunity to turn this penitence into bliss. With malice towards none, I pray to Sai to bless all, with whom I came into contact directly or remotely in all these years, with 'Shraddha' and 'Saburi' (Faith with devotion, along with patience, forbearance and fortitude).

To be in solitude, silence and emotional concentration on the Perfect Master (Sadguru) and the Over-Soul is referred to as 'Ekant' and 'Ananya' bhava. Devotional Love by way of reflecting on and remembering (Manan and Smaran) of His Word (Sabad) and Swarup gives the utmost joy. Romantic loves of yesteryears or other loves in human relationship are not comparable to the Devotional Love, which is long lasting and eternal. Being a devotee of a Sadguru you re-discover your real Self within and re-invent your other worldly relationships all over again. You become less narrow-minded, less self-centred, selfish, egoistic, greedy, passionate and angry, and become more and more magnanimous, compassionate, kind and considerate to others – human beings animals and even inanimate Nature. It looks like your personality has undergone a metamorphosis and transformation for better both within and outside. Life becomes much more meaningful. No longer do petty desires, passions and fears overtake you, and Sattwik gunas remain pre-dominant in your thoughts, emotions, action and conduct. As you gravitate towards Sadguru's Swarup, He takes care of your legitimate needs: 'Yogakshemam Vahamyaham' – to quote the words of the Lord in Srimad Bhagavad Gita. As Shirdi Sai Baba had assured: "You look at Me; I look at You....." What is implied here is total surrender to Him, with your body, mind, property and will. You become a "Gurumukh" (in the words of Holy Adi Granth) in toto – looking exclusively in the direction of Sadguru at all time.... You respond sincerely to the instructions of Lord Krishna in the Gita: "Sarvadharman parityejya mamekam saranam vraja...." (Leaving aside all other paths, take refuge in Me....). You evolve to remain in His Swarupa (likeness), Salokya (Same region), Sampiya (dearest) and Sayujya (Merger) – the four phenomena of liberation. You evolve within from your "Annamaya' kosh (food body) to Pranamaya (pranic body), Manamaya (mental body), Vignanmaya (intuitive body) and Anandamaya Kosh (bliss body) to be immersed in 'Brahmananda', and 'Purushakar' – God realized soul – the ultimate goal of life.

You do not merely exist – you live purposefully. It is no longer going on the usual path of Samsarik material life of repetitions or chewing the chewed (Poonah Poonah Charvita Charvanam). You live with the taste of the elixir of Divine Love and Ecstasy, which is 'Amrit Swarup'. You get intoxicated with the 'Wine of Divine Love' at all time, becoming part of Immortality. Death for you takes on a new meaning and dimension – you become fearless, as your Sadguru plays His role in smoothening your process of dying – before, during and after your physical death. The painful transitions in the cycle of birth and death become painless and joyful. Same is the case with the other two afflictions of old age and disease, as well as the three-some sufferings (adhi bhautik, adhi daivik and adhyatmik)......

It is the Time then to celebrate Eternal Existence, Consciousness and Bliss (Satchidananda).

Part - I
Life's Gross Journey

1

Birth, Parentage, Brothers and Sisters

I was born on the 8th day in the dark fortnight of the month of Chaitra before sunrise in the year 1941 (19th March as per the Gregorian calendar) in Tigiria village in the native princely State of Tigiria (now part of Cuttack district in Odisha State of India). My father, Shri Janardana Nanda, a native of Dhenkanal (a neighbouring princely state), was working as the doctor-in-charge of Tigiria Hospital. My mother, Binodini, had already given birth to four daughters. The birth of a son after four daughters was welcomed by all, and I received unusual care and attention.

My father hailed from a lower middle class family of indigenous medical practitioners (Vaidyas) and Sanskrit scholars (Pandits) with the clan title 'Nanda' in a forest village of 'Mandukhura', now in Kamakhyanagar subdivision of Dhenkanal district. From a family lineage tree maintained by my father, I could know that our forefathers had come from Kanauj region of Uttar Pradesh centuries back to a village,

'Osana Barpada' in Kanas Block of Puri district on the invitation of the King of Puri to serve Lord Jagannath both as Sanskrit scholars and spiritual healers. One branch of the family later migrated to Dhenkanal.

My father's father (Balakrushna Nanda) – a Vaidya had died when my father was in school and his mother, Sunadevee, had died in his childhood. His two elder brothers (Maheshwar and Trilochan) had also met with untimely death. My father could not go for higher university education, but pursued the study of medicine in Cuttack Medical School, where he completed his education as an LMP doctor topping in both surgery and medicine. He sacrificed an offer of higher education abroad to take responsibility of a big joint family of his brother's children and his widowed elder sister from a child marriage (who stayed in our house till her death in 1982). He joined as a doctor in Bhuban hospital near his village, and got married in Mishra family of Talcher (another neighbouring Princely State). My maternal grandfather, Narayan Mishra was the civil engineer of Talcher State, and was associated with the designs of many bridges including the repair of Howrah Bridge in Kolkata. My mother had two brothers and four sisters. She studied up to Class-VI, but was proficient in Odia and Bengali languages and literature. My mother's two brothers (Haraprasad and Durgaprasad) and four sisters (Sulakhyana, Saudamini, Subhagini and Laxmipriya) had in all 24 sons and 19 daughters, most of whom have established themselves in prominent positions in life, and some of them have settled abroad. Three of my cousins – Sarat Mishra, Pyarimohan Mahapatra and Bipin Behari Mishra – were members of all-India services. My eldest cousin, Brajabandhu Mishra, was Professor of Mathematics and held important positions in educational administration. Some of my other elder cousins – Shyamabandhu, Gopabandhu, Jagabandhu, Sashibhusan, Murli Mohan, Lalitmohan, Rudra Mohan, Rabindra Nath, Binod Bihari and Prashant Kumar – were very fond of me. So also were my younger cousins – Golakh, Bhagavatiprasad, Devi Prasad, Bhavaniprasad, Dhabal and a few others.

My father became very well-known as a doctor in Dhenkanal, but had to leave the place due to the eccentric behaviour of the king. After a brief stint of private practice at Cuttack town, he came to Tigiria in 1936 on the invitation of the king to open an allopathic hospital. My first two sisters were born in Dhenkanal, but all other brothers and sisters (including me) were born in Tigiria.

My father's elder sister, Budhei nani, was a widow soon after her marriage in childhood and continued to stay with us till her death in 1982. She was very caring of all of us and stood by my parents in all crisis situations. As children, we loved the traditional culinary delicacies she used to prepare at home. I remember the special food (Habisyanna) she used to prepare during the month of Kartik for her evening meal (the only meal). I used to recite one chapter from the Bhagavad Purana and Kartik Purana every evening, and she would feed me with the special dishes which I liked. My cousins (children of father's elder brother, Trilochan Nanda) were staying off and on with us during my childhood. Rajkishore – my eldest cousin – worked as an LIC officer, lost two wives and married for the third time. Other elder cousins – Dhaneshwar, a Sanskrit pundit and teacher; Birakishore, a police officer, who retired as Dy. SP; Suryamani, a senior school teacher; and Shashibhusan, a mining engineer with Tatas – have all retired. The first three and the last one are no more, and the remaining one (Surya Mani) is settled at Cuttack. The eldest cousin sister, Indu Nani, who is in her early 90s, is staying at Dhenkanal with her daughter. The other cousin sister, Nisha Nani died a long time back.

My eldest sister, Snehalata, and the next one, Premlata, were married off just before completing their M.E. education. They were very affectionate and caring towards me in my childhood. Snehalata, who has settled down in Dhenkanal (marrying Krushnamohan – an advocate) faced a series of tragedies in her life with the untimely death of her eldest son Pradeep and three sons-in-law. Now, in her early 80s, she is quite alert and courageous. One of her sons, Pravas, has risen to the rank of Director of Central Cancer Institute of Railways at Varanasi and is now working as the Medical Superintendent of Kalinga Hospital in Bhubaneshwar.

My next elder sister, Premlata, who used to live at Puri with her husband (Radhabinod – a retired Education Officer) and the youngest son, completely devoted to worship of Lord Jagannath, breathed her last in July, 2013. Her two sons (Pramod and Prabodh) and two daughters (Minati and Elu) are settled in the USA with their families. I used to make it a point to visit them during some of my US trips. My love for music got its initial fillip in childhood from Prema nani. I recollect the first few songs in Hindi I used to sing:

'Ab tere siwa kaun mera Krishna, Kanhaiya....'
'Jiya bekrar hai, chai bahar hai'
'Gae ja Geet Milan ke'...

I had also learnt many old Odia songs (Champu and Odissi).

My third elder sister, Bidyutlata, was a meritorious student and taught me subjects of High School in advance, as I passed the M.E. school and enabled me to be a topper in class. While I was studying in 6th and 7th classes in Ravenshaw Collegiate School at Cuttack, she and my immediate elder sister, Shantilata, were studying at Ravenshaw Girls' School at Cuttack. We were staying with our father and uncle's family in a rented house at Mehendipur, where my sisters used to cook food for us, while I helped them in some way. We would walk to and from the school as we could not afford the rickshaw. Bidyutlata passed matriculation, and we all came back to our native village. After two years, she got married to Saurava Nanda – a police intelligence Officer, and had three sons – Dipak (a Doctor), Kunmuna (Advocate) and Alok (Chartered

Accountant) and one daughter Lilima – all of them well-settled. She pursued her higher studies after marriage, ending with an M.A. in English literature to become a lecturer in the Christ College, Cuttack. She wrote short stories, novels, biography and translations; but died in April 2007, a few years after her husband's death.

My fourth elder sister Shantilata studied up to M.A. and Ph.D. in Sanskrit, married Rabi Tripathy – an agricultural scientist and a Sahitya Academy awardee and taught at a college. I studied in the same class with her in school from class-2 onwards, and we used to share one set of books. Rabi babu is now engrossed in spiritual literature.

My younger brothers and sisters have all studied up to graduate or post graduate levels; two of them (Charu and Reeta – both sisters) are now settled in Canada and the USA, respectively, and all others (Santosh, Lalit, Taru, Niru, Iru and Sushil) are settled around Bhubaneswar – Cuttack – Tigiria in Odisha. Most of them are now associated with the Shirdi Sai Charitable and Spiritual Trust, Tigiria, under whose auspices, a Shirdi Sai temple has come up. The day-to-day management of the Temple at Tigiria is entrusted to my youngest brother, Sushil and his wife, Mamta, who teaches at Athgarh Women's College nearby. All other brothers and sisters, along with their spouses have retired from service, and their children are all working, mostly in the private sector. Charu (my younger sister), who was a brilliant student of M.Sc. in Botany, married a scientist, Nalin Hota and migrated to Canada immediately after her marriage in late 1968. She has three daughters – Sheila, Sonia and Sussie. She lost her husband in the late 1980s and later married Lalu Mansingh, a geo-physicist in the University of Western Ontario at London Ontario, where they are settled now. Lalu is the eldest son of the eminent Odia writer, Mayadhara Mansingh, and takes active interest in Indo-Canadian Collaborative studies, research and development projects in Odisha, like the Kalinga Hospital and Buddhist circuit. My youngest sister, Reeta, migrated to the USA after her marriage with Sudhakar Mishra (a Mathematics Professor) in the early '80s. Sudhakar has been teaching and researching in New York and is an avid reader of spiritual literature and philosophy. They have three sons (Sambit, Sandip and Dipu) and one daughter, Sangeeta.

My two younger brothers, Santosh (a mechanical engineer) and Lalit (a legal professional) have worked in Odisha Lift Irrigation Corporation and State Financial Corporation, respectively. Santosh's wife, Basanti, retired as the Principal of a College. Lalit's wife, Meena, is a prize-winning writer in Odia. Both the brothers are trustees of Shirdi Sai Charitable Trust, Tigiria. Lalit had interest in Odia film acting and direction. He produced a film based on a story written by his wife. Santosh has two daughters (Rosy and Jollu) and Lalit has only one daughter, Miku. Rosy teaches in Banaras Hindu University along with her husband. Jollu works in Bhubaneshwar and Miku works at Boston (USA) along with her husband. My younger brother, Sushil's two sons are working at Mumbai and Bhubaneshwar, respectively. His eldest son, Guddu, who is working as a special effect film producer in Bollywood and has bagged a national film award for his work, is now married.

My younger sister, Niru is married to Madhusudan, who retired as MD, Odisha Agro Industry Corporation. Another younger sister, Iru is married to Durga Madhav, who retired recently as a Philosophy Professor and Principal of a College. Niru has two sons working in Odisha and Iru has one son, who is doing his Ph.D at Chandigarh.

My younger sister, Tarulata was emotionally the closest with my wife, Manorama, and continues to give intimate emotional support to my three daughters after my wife's untimely demise in 1990. She is a Ph.D. in History and taught in colleges at Rourkela (where her husband, Rudra Dwivedy, worked at the Steel Plant, retiring as a Deputy General Manager) and later at Bhubaneshwar. She is a sincere Sai devotee and is actively involved in the management of Sai temple along with Rudra and social service. She is an epitome of selfless service and vivacity just as my dear wife Manorama was. She is the dearest aunt to my three daughters, Bijayalaxmi, Upali and Lita, and dearest grand aunt to their children, particularly Akshara, Akanksha and Adarsh and visits them frequently in Delhi. Her two sons, Soumya Kant and Chandra Kant are married and settled in jobs at Gurgaon and Bhubaneshwar, respectively.

2

Childhood and Education

My parents told me that I was handed over symbolically and ritualistically to a mendicant living in an Ashram near my village and given the nick-name 'Babaji' for detachment and longevity, as I was an ailing child with threat to my survival in childhood. I faintly recollect the mendicant taking charge of me every Sunday for a few hours. I remember his smiling face as one of peace, piety and compassion. I have fading memory of the child survival strategy based on faith.

Another such strategy of faith was the unique celebration of each birthday of mine, up to the sixteenth year through night long 'Thia Pala' (Hari Katha like) by a group of artists with dance and music on themes from the Puranas. I used to like the paraphernalia of this art form – the gorgeous dresses of regality, musicals and stories – but did not understand the spiritual-ethical aspects. I used to fall asleep as night advanced.

My father's sister and my elder sisters were very caring of me. I remember the wedding of my second elder sister along with the regalia of the Kings of Tigiria and Mandasa (two brothers), who attended the wedding reception. I also remember the marriage procession of the king, who came back with the queen (the bride from Purulia) shortly before India's independence and merger of the princely states.

The exuberance of Independence days and the tragedy of Mahatma Gandhi's death are vivid in my memory along with the transition of the local monarchy into the republic. We, as primary school students were holding small national flags, moving in procession singing patriotic songs and raising slogans. The end of the monarchy (ruling chief) in my village area (Tigiria was the smallest Princely State in British India) had transitional anarchy for a short period, as some self-styled local leaders formed a republic with a mini-cabinet, creating problems for the king's employees. The State Government took prompt measures to control the situation, and formalised the merger of the Princely State into India.

My formal schooling started with Class-2, as I insisted on attending the class of my elder sister, Shantilata. I had learnt the basic reading, writing and counting skills at home under the tutelage of a village teacher-cum-astrologer (Abadhan) and could get over my nervousness of school attendance being with my sister.

The class teacher (Jayakrishna Mishra) was distantly related to our family. He recorded my date of birth as 19 May 1942 (making me one year and two months younger) without asking my parents, for reasons better known to him. He was very caring of students and used to read aloud the newspaper stories on the partition of India, the communal riots, Gandhi, Nehru and Patel. Whenever any school Sub-Inspector visited our school, he would prompt us from the rear through gestures to answer questions. He had physical disability due to filarial elephantiasis leg; but his enthusiasm never waned, when it came to discussion of national and international news. He lived to see me settling down in the Indian Administrative Service, and expressed his pride at my achievement in life. For one year during my primary schooling, I had to study in another school at Baramba (not very far from Tigiria), as my father was transferred there. There I made new friends like Mrutunjaya, Shiva and Sadasiv, of whom Mrutunjaya remained in regular contact through our college days and later. I did not feel very comfortable in another school and was very happy to come back to the earlier village school after a year where I passed the Primary school examination in 1949, and joined Class-4 in the M.E. School in Tigiria. For the next two years, I studied here securing third rank in the annual examination with Akulananda Bastia and Arakshit Sahoo securing the first two positions. My phobia for Arithmetic had taken roots in my mind, and I was not doing well in this subject.

My father took premature voluntary retirement from the State Medical Service, and started private practice at Cuttack (with two days of practice at Tigiria every week). I was luckily selected for admission in Class-VI in the premier school of Odisha – Ravenshaw Collegiate, Cuttack, where I studied for the next two years. The high teaching standard in this school built a very strong foundation for my career in the high school in my village, where I had to come back, as my father shifted his practice to Dhenkanal-Athagarh-Tigiria. This looked like a foolish step, as I was giving a go-bye to the prestigious school at Cuttack, where many prominent personages, like Netaji Subhas Bose had studied and which had two or three toppers in the best ten every year consistently in the school final examination in the state for years. In my village, the non-government high school was fairly new, and was bristled with many problems including the building (mud-mortar thatched one) and lack of teaching staff. Some of the students like me, who were living close by or in hostel, were expected to clean the floor with cow dung on Sundays. The few teachers, who taught us, were paid their salaries once in three to six months. But they were very dedicated and honest, and were trying to give their best. We were trying very hard to study. My elder sister, Bidyutlata helped me a lot in my efforts. I was securing first or second positions in the class, and was aiming to secure a First Division. The first three batches in the school had a few passing in Second Division and the majority in third division. In the year 1957, when our batch appeared in the school leaving examination, two of us (Antaryami Panda and me) got First Division, and to the surprise and disbelief of everyone including me (my father was the only exception, who was predicting from the housetop, much to my discomfiture, about my chance of being in the top ten), I secured the second position in the entire State.

In fact, a new record of a sort was set when the top two positions among the best ten went to the relatively unknown non-government schools in remote rural areas, and not to the premier Ravenshaw Collegiate or any of the urban government schools, which used to monopolise most of the top ten positions. My friend and colleagues in IAS Odisha cadre, Sahadeva Sahoo stood first studying from a rural school in Jajpur area, and I followed him closely (with two marks less). I secured overwhelmingly high marks in all subjects except in Mathematics (averaging 85 per cent) and Science (with just 51 per cent). Such an astonishing achievement, I attribute to the inspiration and guidance from my teachers (like Nabakishore Dash, Narayan Dash and Khageshwar Mahapatra), my father and elder sister and, above all, to the bountiful Grace of God.

Towards the end of my schooling and the beginning of college education, I was drawn to Marxism, Communist movement and students' federation on the one hand, and to romantic literature, philosophical and historical writings on the other. In between these two romantic proclivities, I liked to read books of Swami Sivananda (Divine Life Society) and Shree Ramakrishna Mission. I opted for study in the Humanities and Arts stream in Intermediate classes in the premier Ravenshaw College at Cuttack with Economics, History and Logic as subjects. I stayed in West Hostel for four years. I retained a First Division in I.A. Examination with a third position in the state, and continued in the same college in B.A. with Honours in Political Science and History as the pass subject. The Government of India Merit scholarship of Rs. 50/- per month in I.A. and Rs. 75/- per month in B.A. was keeping me financially stable. Taking a subject like 'Political Science' was a decision guided by consideration of well-wishers that it was the most likely way of getting selected for the administrative service – an idea, which took roots in the psyche of the middle class with upward aspiration for power, prestige and position in society. My earlier ambition to serve the poor by becoming a doctor, or later ambition to be a romantic dreamer, thinker and philosopher by taking literature and philosophy came to naught. I chose the more pragmatic path, much to the satisfaction of my parents and elders.

In my school days in the village, I was occasionally engaged in overseeing agricultural operations on the land of my father. I learnt the art of seed sowing, planting, weeding and harvesting of paddy cultivation as well as fish catching from the agricultural labourers working in the fields. I took keen interest in vegetable growing in our kitchen garden in the home backyard as well as in the school orchard. Besides, I took part in games like kabaddi, volleyball and football in the school.

I remember the princely state raj days during my early childhood, when the king's elephant would come to our house every Sunday for remote village visits of my father as a doctor. I used to feed the elephant with bananas, and the mahunt would take me for the elephant ride to a short distance.

We had no electricity in our area and had to study at home in the evenings with kerosene lantern. I had the first experience of electrical light and fan when I came to Cuttack to study in class-VI. Our village was electrified after I passed my M.A. But street electricity eludes this village even today. We now miss the dense forest, foliage, snakes and wild life including tigers, which we were accustomed to see or encounter in those days as a child. The fear of man-eater tigers in winter nights is now a thing of the past.

As I was transiting through my late adolescence, as is the wont, I went through emotional turbulence. Although I was very sincere, conscientious and regular in my studies in the college, and stayed away from torrid romantic adventurism of some of my classmates, I was silently and inadvertently drawn into a romantic platonic relationship of sort, which disturbed my equipoise and concentration in study to a considerable extent. Through intensive day dreaming, symbolic romantic outbursts through poetry and music, and occasional exchange of pleasantries, I wove around this platonic relationship a beautiful emotional life, which has given positive and multi-coloured facets to life in the long run. On the whole, it has taught me to sublimate human relationships in more positive and even spiritual directions.

I quote a few ghazals (English rendering) to reflect emotions around the first love of adolescence:-

"How I rue my lingering on in our first meeting
And the encouragement she gave me through her greeting.
You will never like it to end if you hear carefully my heart's story.
Shooting arrow after arrow, she would say
"Had you taken love for a child's play?"

(Amir Meenai, translated by K. Salil)

"Every plant and every petal my condition knows
Only the flower knows not, the entire garden knows...
Nobody in the world can be as simple as a lover
When in love, his heart's enemy, his god does he consider..."

(Meer Taqi Meer)

"To the fraternity of lovers,
God knows what's happening
They know neither the art of living
Nor do they know the art of dying.
The tragedy in love took place a long age ago
But I hear the sound of your pounding heart even now..."

(Jigar Muradabadi, translated by Kuldip Salil)

"She touched my life-string
And hid away somewhere.
Her voice only, now I hear...
On hearing which the whole mehfil into raptures went....
It was the voice of a broken instrument...

(Majaz Lukhnavi, translated by Kuldip Salil)

Staying away from home comforts in a college hostel had its own take. Community life away from family environment brought in trials and tribulations with homesickness for some time. Acquiring friends, and getting engaged in student union activities built a new personality with fellow feeling, camaraderie and self confidence. I started reading one English newspaper – *The Statesman* daily, and took initiative along with others to start a 'Literary Mazlis', a circle of like-minded students, where we would invite notable Odia writers and critics to speak. I helped in the editing of the hostel magazine, *Urmi*. I used to write a few literary pieces including poems in the college journal, *Ravenshavian*. I was quite shy of public speaking, but started joining the college debating society. Most of the college teachers and the Principal were appreciative of my curricular performance, except one (Prof. Sriram Chandra Dash), who was prone to autocracy, sycophancy and favouritism, and did not like my independent attitude. He never forgot the fact that I was elected by overwhelming majority to the post of Secretary of Political Science Association in my third year B.A., defeating his nominee, Rajendra Narayan Dash (who has retired as an IAS officer of Bihar Cadre). He also went to the extent of manipulating my marks in some papers to ensure that I did not get a First Class in Honours in the B.A. final examination. He went to the extent of declaring from the housetop that he will hang himself in the nearest lamp-post if I got into the Indian Administrative Service. This Professor proclaimed later that he was very proud of my achievement. I hold him in high esteem for his oratory and memory power.

Failing to get a First Class Honours in B.A. (falling short by two marks) meant my losing the Government of India merit scholarship of Rs.100/- per month for my post-graduate study. I did not want to continue my post graduate study in Utkal University, as the same teacher, who used to hold a grudge against me, was going to be the Professor and Head of the Faculty. I, therefore, went to Allahabad University in U.P. for my postgraduate study. Allahabad University was rated then as the best in teaching standard and the most suitable for success in all-India services competitive examination. Subjects like Political Science in Allahabad held out promise for such success year after year. The teaching faculty was excellent with stalwarts like A. B. Lal, A.D. Pant and Mohan Lal, who were impeccably honest, impartial, unbiased and inspiring. Going from Odisha to the environment of Allahabad was like breathing fresh air. A few of my friends from Odisha also came there to study. I stayed in Sir P.C. Banerjee Hostel, where some of us started an Eastern India Mess for getting food of our choice. Some of us had a trip to Chitrakoot area and saw many places of pilgrimage, under the leadership of my senior Achyuta Nanda Mishra (who has retired as professor in Utkal University).

I actively participated in seminars, debates and literary competitions, and got some awards. I participated in music programme of group songs (Bharat Bhuin repuji amere) under the direction of my friend Bidhu Samanta (who topped in M.Com and has retired as a senior UNICEF officer. Bidhu has contributed liberally to the construction of Shirdi Sai temple at my village. Another soul mate of mine, Prafulla Das, who topped in M.A. (Previous) in Political Science, joined the Gujarat cadre of IAS and is settled at Gandhinagar. Pyarimohan (my cousin) and R.K. Bhujabal (both 1963 batch IAS Odisha Cadre) were my mentors. Niladri Mahanty (who became an officer in the State Bank of India later) was helpful during my days of emotional turbulence in Allahabad. So was Dipak Mishra (who joined Indian Foreign Service later and is no more). Babu

Mahapatra, Bullu Das, Fakir Panda, Subhendu Mahanty, Lal Birendra Shahdeo, S.N. Tewari, Bidhu Samanta, Ramji Lal Patwari, Prasanna Mishra, Prateep Mahanty, Swadesh Datta and many other friends were studying in the same university.

I passed M.A. in mid 1963, and stayed in a rented house at Church Lane, Allahabad along with my friend, Prafulla Das, preparing for the Civil Services Examination in the same year from Allahabad Centre. Both of us were called for interview for the posts of lecturer in Political Science in Utkal University, and became successful despite opposition from the same Professor, who shunted us to Evening Colleges, instead of permitting us to join the main campus in the Post Graduate Faculty for which we were recruited.

Some of my friends from student (school, college or university) days, with whom there has been frequent contact and interaction are Dolagobinda Panda (retired Professor of Political Science), Mrutyunjaya Patnaik (retired Chief Engineer), Antaryami Panda (retired Engineer-in-Chief), Digambar Mishra (Professor and Dean in USA), Madhu Sudan Pati (topped in M.A. English and became an eminent professor in Sambalpur University), Baishnab Charan Das (retired as reader of Political Science), Trilochan Kanungo (an eminent political leader), S.M. Raffique (LIC Agent), Samarendra Kumar Mahapatra (retired General Insurance G.M.), Md. Ayoob (Professor in the USA), Gyana Kar (retired Professor), Gopinath Das (retired Chief Engineer), Rajendra Das (Germany). I have been interacting with some eminent seniors from my village area like Prof. Debiprasanna Patnaik (eminent linguist), Laxmi Dhar Tunga (administrator) and Hemant Kumar Das (retired as Director of Treasuries), as well as village school friends, such as Lalit Patnaik, Banabehari Patnaik, Purna Dash and Durga Das.

3

Early Working Career (1964-1974)

My working life began on 1 January 1964 at Berhampur town in south Odisha as a lecturer of Political Science in the Utkal University Evening College. I stayed in a rented house along with another colleague, Radhanath Rajguru (who joined the Orissa Administrative Service later) and we used to cook our food. Most of the students were employed in jobs, and it was a tough job to keep their interest in the lectures going, as they were very tired after their day's work. I tried to make my lectures interesting and hopefully most of them were not dozing off. I did not continue with my teaching job for more than six months, as I qualified in the civil services examination for Central Services and Indian Police Service by May, 1964. My viva voce examination at Kolkata in April, 1964 went off well even though I had just recovered from paratyphoid fever and escaped a train accident, where many people died or sustained injuries near Bhadrak town.

I joined the Indian Revenue Service (Income tax) in early July, 1964 on probation for a five month long foundational course at the National Academy of Administration at Mussoorie Hill Station. About 500 young colleagues join you from all over India (and even one from Bhutan) on a journey in the top civil services for almost 35 years or so. This year was the last such combined foundational course and from next year, the batch was divided into two courses. Mr. Dutt was the Academy director. He belonged to the ICS and was a very liberal administrator. He gave us utmost freedom to enjoy our new found success. Suddenly you feel on the top of the world tasting success. You are the most sought after in the society, particularly in the marriage market.

My platonic romance of college days had already come to a tragic-comic end, as the girl did not wait for my hand in marriage and married somewhere else! It became like a story of a Hindi movie on unrequited love of those days. I was consoled by my friends as a tragic hero, and the impression remains etched in their memory to this day.

The lingering shadows of memories could be best described in the language of two ghazals I am quoting below:

"There is neither the flood of memories now, nor are there
long dull days of leisure.
Only a little anguish remains in the heart,
No longer the deep wound that was there"

(Nasir Qazmi, translated by Kuldip Salil)

"For a long time now, I have not
had the luxury of weeping.
Come and make me cry, O my comforter,
If else for nothing
I still have illusion, I still have
hope from you.
Come and blow out this last candle too"...

(Ahmed Faraz, translated by Kuldip Salil)

Life in Mussoorie Academy was regal. They prepare you to build a strong foundation of an administrative leader in fairly senior positions in your job from the beginning. You get integrated into the system and are expected to lead people, who may be much older or senior in age and more experienced and knowledgeable.

Some of us in IPS or central services, who had the chance to sit for IAS/IFS examination, were permitted to do so in a special centre at the Academy in October, 1964, and I was one of them. In December, 1964, I went to the Income Tax Officer's Training College at Nagpur, where I underwent training till June, 1965. We had a very pleasant stay at Nagpur, where I learnt guitar and Rabindra Sangeet for a while. A few of us qualified finally to join the IAS – the premier service, and I joined the same in July, 1965.

I was allotted my own State Odisha as my cadre, and was instructed to join the State Training Academy at Hirakud, as I had already done six months at Mussoorie the previous year. A frustrated senior bureaucrat, who was the Principal of this training institute, did not behave properly with us and exhibited his ego and eccentricity by extending the training period for some of us till October, 1965. Our training in the IAS started with a bang, leaving a feeling of hurt for some time.

As I went to Mussoorie Academy in November, 1965, I found that the atmosphere there had changed completely compared to the serene and pleasant days of 1964. The new Director, Mr. Pimputkar – an ICS officer of impeccable honesty – was a hyper-disciplinarian and eccentric person, who had instilled fear and suspicion in the minds of the probationers. The 1965 batch of the combined civil services, having been broken into two batches for training, some of us who went late, could not integrate well into the group of the fresh entrants, who had joined in July. This feeling remains until today whenever we meet in the 1965 batch get-togethers, unlike the bonhomie, bonding and integration of the 1964 batch.

My marriage to Manorama, betrothed in May, 1965, took place in December, 1965. Mr. R.P. Khosla, the Deputy Director permitted me a fortnight's leave for marriage, much to the chagrin of the Director, Mr. Pimputkar, who chided me for having broken the unwritten code of discipline. I was penalized by very low marks in the 'personality' column of the report, for which I came down by a few positions in the inter-se rank in the batch. This is the price one pays for breaking the Director's diktat on marriage! This was my first experience of the 'steel frame' of the civil service.

Some of us belonging to Odisha cadre, who knew Odia and Bengali, were required to study Telugu and pass a test before leaving Mussoorie. Our Telugu teacher had given us some probable questions, and we did our preparation accordingly. One of our batch mates was studying his notes outside the examination hall, even when half an hour had elapsed, and his notes were taken away to the Director, who came to the conclusion that the question paper had been leaked. Our test was scrapped. We were asked to reappear after one year. Some of us suffered by way of delayed confirmation and senior scale promotion. The Telugu test was finally exempted by the Government after public agitation and Assembly discussions in Odisha.

The most pleasant memory of Mussoorie days was Bharat Darshan (all-India tour) and the Kashmir trip including the army attachment. Our group covered Delhi, Rajasthan, Madhya Pradesh, Gujarat, Maharashtra, Andhra, Tamil Nadu, Karnataka and Kerala. In a short period, we were exposed to many facets of Pan Indian culture and history. We were given short orientation in civil defence, rural development and weapon training (in forward areas of Kashmir). The tour from the Poonch sector of Indo-Pak border to Kanyakumari was an exhilarating experience indeed!

As I left Mussoorie end-June, 1966, I was posted for practical training in Koraput district of Odisha as Assistant Collector and Magistrate. My wife, Manorama, joined me there and I was allotted a small house in a Government colony close to a dense forest. As an Assistant Collector, one is expected to learn the practical work of the District and sub-district units of administration, ranging from the basic treasury and accounting to land revenue, development, social welfare, excise, mining, forestry, agriculture and allied sector, survey, land records and settlement, as well as judicial magistracy, law and order etc. One has to interact with, observe and learn from variegated departmental officers, technocrats, judges and judicial magistrates and other heads of district administration. The District Magistrate and Collector is supposed to guide you in all this. I got a calendar of training drawn up for a few months. I meticulously went through the training programme, maintained a detailed diary and submitted case records to the District Judge. I underwent survey and land records settlement training in Phulbani-Ganjam districts (at Katingia and Parlakhemundi). I stayed in Circuit Houses, Inspection Bungalows, Rest Sheds and sometimes in tents. A tiger once jumped over one of the tents in Katingia survey camp, and I saw bears and herds of elephants on the forest path. Walking on foot or riding bicycles was enjoyable. On the whole, life was enjoyable and adventurous as I went through the nitty-gritty of practical grassroots administration. One comes to know the problems of grassroots workers and the common man. The insight I gained and the tricks of the trade I learnt in the field built a solid foundation and an ethos for the next 36 years of my public service career. I am grateful to all those colleagues/senior or subordinates) who trained me to become a useful member of the I.A.S. It is not possible to name all of them. Some of them are B.M. Padhi, (Collector, Koraput), D.P. Tripathy (Collector, Puri), S.K. Basu (ADM, Ganjam), M.P. Modi (ADM, Puri), V.K. Samantaray (Settlement Officer), D.P. Mohanty (ADM, Koraput), B.B. Jena (ADM, Koraput), N.K. Mishra (Treasury Officer), I.C. Das, Dwijabar Kanungo, Bijaya Kumar Dasand and many more....

My Block and Tahsil training took place in Sakhigopal and Bhubaneshwar, respectively in Puri district. The hands-on work of a BDO and Tahsildar for a few months towards the end of the training period was very interesting. I passed the written and oral tests on revenue laws conducted by the Board of Revenue. I had taken very keen interest in survey, land records and settlement training. Maybe, that was the reason why I got my first independent substantive posting after training in October, 1967 as Settlement Charge Officer, Ganjam – Koraput Major Settlement at Berhampur – the place where I had started my working career as a University teacher. All my other batch-mates in Odisha cadre were posted as Sub-divisional Officers with the perks, power and prestige, which is denied to a Settlement Charge Officer. However, I enjoyed every bit of my work, even though I had to stay in a rented house and travel in public transport.

One builds expertise and better knowledge supervising survey and land record settlement operation, which is the core of the land administration affecting majority of the common man, particularly in the rural area. This came to me in good stead in my appreciation of population and development issues later on.

My Parlakhemundi Days (1968-1970)

By mid-1968, I was transferred and posted as Sub-divisional Officer, Parlakhemundi in Ganjam district bordering Srikakulam of Andhra Pradesh. This subdivision is now a full fledged 'Gajapati' district. I spent two years in this subdivision, even as I was promoted to senior scale and re-designated as 'Sub-Collector' for some time. The major part of the subdivision comprised hills and dense forests inhabited mostly by tribals (Sauras and Khonds) in two Tahsils (Parlakhemundi and R. Udaygiri) and seven Blocks. The district headquarters was far away at Chhatrapur, and hence, the SDO was virtually a collector here. I worked very hard, gave my heart and soul for the betterment of the people, and loved my work.

The exploitive situation leading to utter poverty of the tribals was what struck me as the problem number one. My pro-left pro-poor leaning from school days impelled me from within to take the cudgels of power and law to strike at the root – the issue of unlawful transfer of land of tribals to non-tribals, and the trap of indebtedness and cheating. The laws were enforced strictly, and justice was delivered at the doorstep of the tribals through frequent camp courts held by me. The land was restored to tribals, and police was asked to enforce this. I was lucky to have senior police officers with dynamism like Bibhutibhusan Nandy, who helped proactively in this regard. The big traders and money lenders were very unhappy and pulled strings with politicians to get us transferred. The Deputy Chief Minister, Pabitra Mohan Pradhan, who visited the subdivision and addressed 'Clean Administration' meetings at each Block for a week, lauded our efforts and impressed upon Chief Minister, R.N. Singhdeo, not to shift me.

The first wave of Naxalite movement (of Charu Majumdar's brand) was sweeping Andhra Pradesh and the tribal areas of Odisha during that period. There were reprisal murders of rich traders and money lenders all along the borders of the subdivision in Srikakulam- Tekkali-Vishakhapatnam region. The Naxalite leaders recognized our efforts and declared that they would not create problems in our subdivision. In fact, some of the lawyers and intellectuals with Naxalite or pro-left leanings were helping us in our mission to help the tribals.

I was lucky to have an excellent officer in Jagannath Shroff (who died in March 2015) as Tahsildar, R. Udaygiri. He was a knowledgeable, sincere and honest officer, who assisted me to the hilt in our mission to give the tribals their due. I was equally lucky to have my mentor in Shri Bimal Kishore Mishra (an IAS Officer of 1950 batch), who as the Revenue Divisional Commissioner of Southern Division, encouraged me in my efforts. He was a very knowledgeable, honest and strict officer, who, through his frequent tours of my area and inspection of my work, guided me to shape up in his style of working. He is no more. I bow down my head in respect to this legendary administrator.

Bimal babu had advised me to show due respect to the Maharaja of Parlakhemundi, who was one of the prominent architects of formation of the separate province of Odisha in 1936 and was a progressive ruler of the Estate before its abolition. He somehow did not have good experience of young IAS officers in the past and was opposed to their posting as SDO in his area. I did pay a courtesy call on the Maharaja after my joining, and he invited me for a chat over a cup of tea a couple of times during my tenure. He liked clock-like punctuality, frankness in talk, and was very respectful in his dealings. His advice on irrigation system and agriculture in period of drought came out to be very pragmatic and judicious. He never asked for any personal favour.

Another advice that my mentor, Divisional Commissioner, had given me in the presence of my wife just before my joining the post of SDO was to move with my family and not alone. He had cautioned me in the backdrop of some incident of cupidity with young officers in the past, and the habit of anonymous petitions from the area relating to some influential aristocratic women trying to woo the young officers. It sounded amusing to us at that time; but as the situation unfolded, my mentor's advice came in handy. I think I came out unscathed!

In my over-zealousness to tackle corruption in administration, I made surprise checks and inspections, and assiduously built evidence against the erring staff. Unpleasant action had to be taken sometime. In one instance involving misappropriation of Government cash by a cashier, we had to institute a police case and suspend the officer. Getting wind of this action, the cashier disappeared. The police arrested him from Rourkela, where he was running a taxi business. He was finally convicted with imprisonment. On my request, a special audit of accounts of previous ten years was conducted, and many irregularities came to notice. Later on, I was called upon to explain for some of the irregularities, which I had helped in unearthing. Some senior officers in the Government, who did not like my action, wanted to put me under departmental proceedings. The enquiring officer (Shri B.C. Mathur) gave me a clean chit and lauded my initiative. Shri Mathur was Rev. Divisional Commissioner during the enquiry (Shri Mathur passed away in 2013).

I was very charmed with the scenic beauty of the hills and forests and made it a point to explore the flatbed of 'Mahendragiri', the second highest hill in Odisha at 4923 feet above sea level, which had historical pilgrimage tourism potential. I visited Mahendragiri a couple of times, spending a night of Sivaratri in a tent with my wife. We tried to construct a make-shift ghat road up to the hilltop. Collecting from mythological, hagiographical and historical sources, and based on my experience, I ventured to write an article on the importance of Mahendragiri as a place of tourist interest and hill station in the prominent daily newspaper, 'Samaj'.

Many people had interacted with me and helped me in many ways, during those days. I recollect the role of Sub-divisional Police Officers, B.B. Nandy, B.B. Singh and Purna Senapati. There were others, like Binod Lal Padhi (ADPRO) with his bilingual comic humour and negotiating skill, Kora (jeep driver) Ghasi (peon) Bapahati, Padhi, Murthy and Rao (Advocates), Kurmanaikulu (MLA), B.C. Mohanty, (Sub-divisional medical officer) and Saurindra Bose (DFO).

My Sambalpur Days (1970-1972)

After two years of very satisfying job, I moved from Parlakhemundi in southern Odisha to Sambalpur in north-western Odisha on transfer as Additional District Magistrate in May, 1970. I remained in this post for close to two years, working as adjuncts to two District Magistrates in quick succession (P.K. Dey and Sanujit Ghose), who had liberally delegated much of their power and functions. For a few months, when one DM went on leave, I officiated as DM I had the chance to discharge regulatory and statutory duties, hearing quasi-judicial revenue appeals in Court, as well as reviewing and supervising revenue, excise and law and order work. I also worked for coordinating, reviewing and inspecting development programmes in the district.

I was very particular on routine inspections of subordinate offices, like Sub-divisional, Tehsil, Block and Police Stations. I had learnt the meticulous style of inspection from my mentor, Bimal Mishra, and employed it with zest and a sense of positive purpose, which the subordinate colleagues never disliked. I took them in full confidence and sought their opinion at every stage. The notes were not much of fault-finding, but were suggestive of possible improvement.

Reserving some time for public hearing was invariably a part of such inspection visit. My family (wife, two daughters who were born by then, my mother and younger sister Taru) accompanied me in some of the tours, particularly those involving visits to wild life sanctuaries, natural reserves or pilgrimages. The Hirakud reservoir, Gandhamardan hill, Ushakothi sanctuary were places of attraction.

Once I accompanied the Revenue Divisional Commissioner, Shri Gopal Chandra Dash, on an inspection tour of two days to the newly formed Padampur subdivision. He was quite relaxed in his work and was very fond of good food and card game. After the day's work (he inspected the sub-divisional office, while I did the Tahsil office), he got three card players, which included the local Police Inspector (who was related to my wife). His appetite was proverbial, and his stories predicting the deluge of the world were hilarious!

The Raja of the ex-state of Bamra was an MLA then; he invited me and the local SDO during one of my visits to Deogarh for dinner in his palace. He laid out dinner around midnight and did not eat himself, as it was too early for him. He had a peculiar habit of going to bed around 2 a.m. and getting up by 10 a.m. when a big torch of rising sun would be shown to him from the window. He became a Minister in the State after some time.

The feeling of Cuttacki-Sambalpuri (regional hatred) prevalent in Sambalpur was a phenomenon I was aware of, and I took special care to endear myself to them. I had a feeling that they accepted me as one of them.

As the District Election Officer, I had the privilege of conducting the 1971 general election to the Parliament and State Assembly. I became well-equipped with the drills of the election process including decisions of logistics, selection of personnel, their training, and the election laws and regulations. Many national and State political leaders came for campaigning. They included Indira Gandhi, whom I received in a small decrepit airstrip near Jharsuguda. The same Mrs. Gandhi, I saw off (as Divisional Commissioner) in her last visit to Odisha at Bhubaneshwar airport in 1984, just the evening before the day she was assassinated. I had also received her once at Konark during 1976 (as District Magistrate, Puri), when she visited the Konark Sun temple along with her two sons, Rajiv and Sanjay.

The Election Commissioner of India invited all District Election Officers along with the State Chief Electoral Officers to an all India conference at Delhi towards the end of 1971. Suggestions were elicited from us for electoral reforms based on our experience and understanding. I took this opportunity to bring to Delhi my wife and eldest daughter. We stayed for a few days after the conference and visited places like the Red Fort and Qutab Minar. I remember walking all the steps upto the top of the Minar with my wife, while my daughter Bizee was left in the care of the parents of one of my cadre mates of Odisha (Chatrath) on the ground. The climbing up was stopped for the public after some time due to some unfortunate accidents.

I was equally fortunate in conducting the 1971 Housing, Population and Agricultural Census of India, as the designated District Census Officer, Sambalpur. My first initiation into Census was as Sub-divisional Officer during 1969-70, but the real substantive responsibility came, when I was trained by the

State Census Director (Bibhuti Tripathy) at Puri for a few days. It was a pleasure to work under the guidance of Shri Tripathi, who visited my district a couple of times. He picked up a liking for me and wanted to take me as his Senior Deputy Director at the State Census Directorate. This did not materialise. However, I succeeded him in 1979 as the State Director for the 1981 Census, and a decade later in 1989, I was selected to head the Indian Census for the 1991 Census.

My entrenchment and specialization in Census and population studies over the next 40 years of life owes its origin to my interest in Census work in 1970-71 in the Sambalpur district. I visited every nook and corner of the district, supervised all training sessions at sub-divisional and Block levels, and made random inspection of the work in the field. Maps of every village and urban block were prepared, house numbering and listing and population and housing profiles were prepared through a questionnaire by trained enumerators. District Census Handbooks consisting of village and town directories and all relevant statistics were prepared. The 1971 Census Commissioner of India (Chandrasekhar) visited my district.

I had a close encounter with a law and order situation near the Sambalpur college where the students were on strike, and I was negotiating between the striking student leaders and the college authorities for a peaceful settlement. The armed police force led by the Additional S.P. (Nimai Padhi) and the sub-divisional magistrate (Shri Panda) were on the road facing the sloganeering students. Suddenly, there was stone pelting directed towards the police force, who became restive and compelled the magistrate to order the use of force. What followed was a lathi charge after which the crowd was dispersed. Somehow, we averted more use of force, even though some of us (including me) were injured due to the stone pelting. And it was already night. This incident was diffused from conflagrating into a major law and order situation with political fall-out. Due to good rapport between me and

Additional S.P. (N.C. Padhi), it was contained, and some erring police men, who had misbehaved with the SDM, were taken to task. I had good rapport with the college principal and the teaching staff, some of whom (Madhu Sudan Pati, Digambar Mishra and Aditya Padhi) were my classmates in college days.

Along with the SP (D. N. Singh), I made surprise check of inter-state check gate at Sohella, along with a raid on a rice mill at Padampur, and we could unearth illegal and corrupt practices including inter-state smuggling. Such actions were invariably planned carefully and executed with perfect coordination with the senior police officer. The Additional SPs, Ramesh Mahanty and Mathur (both my batch mates in service) were very helpful in co-ordination.

The Chief Secretary, G.C.L. Joneja and Additional Development Commissioner, S.K. Rau, visited the district for review of development projects. Soon after their visit, I received an order of transfer, posting me as Deputy Secretary in Planning and Coordination Department at State Secretariat at Bhubaneshwar (Mr. Joneja died in November, 2013, and S.K. Rau in 2012).

My Bhubaneshwar Days (1972-1975)

I joined the state Planning and Coordination Department in April, 1972 and worked there till the first week of January, 1975. It was considered a key job where one gets a close overview of all sectors of development including inter-sectoral coordination under the direct supervision of two senior most leaders of state bureaucracy (namely, the Chief Secretary and the Additional Development Commissioner). It was an opportunity, a challenge and a risk; but a very fruitful period of learning the State macro plan after my exposure to field implementation at micro level in the district and sub district level. In IAS, one moves up from micro to macro, carrying experience, knowledge and the art of managing and leadership all the way to state level or national level to policy formulation advice at the end.

I had to learn quickly the importance and scope of plan schemes and programmes of all Departments from Agriculture and allied sector to the Welfare of Scheduled Castes and Scheduled Tribes, and even Statistics and Evaluation. Also, one had to understand the mechanism and process of Plan formulation, monitoring and evaluation from the national plan down to the district plan, from the perspective plan to Five-Year Plan down to Annual Plan exercises.

I had to put in long hours of work to be up to date in review reports, plan formulation as per schedule, and plan discussion at State and National Planning Commissions, under the ever watchful eyes of two successive workaholic senior bureaucrats – Dr. S.K. Rau of 1948 batch of IAS (he died in December 2012) and Mr. Bimal Mishra (my earlier mentor). Both of them were hard task masters, but liked my work on the whole. I had to maintain a balanced buffer between the Chief Secretary and Additional Development Commissioner on one side and the Secretaries and Heads of Departments (mostly my seniors) on the other. I tried my best to present their viewpoints and alibi for shortfalls and deficiencies, along with what I considered within my limited knowledge and experiences as unbiased and objective comments. I had to receive brickbats and bouquets from both the sides. In this exercise, I was ably assisted by some junior colleagues, among whom I would like to make special mention of Ganeshwar Mishra, the Under-secretary (He died in January, 1997), who was a veritable memory bank of the history of each Plan scheme since the very First Five Year Plan.

My very first trip by air was in 1972, when I visited Delhi as a part of State Government team for annual Plan discussion in the Planning Commission. There was no direct flight then from Bhubaneshwar to Delhi; we had to go to Calcutta (now Kolkata) by a small turbo engine flight, and then take a bigger flight to Delhi after waiting at Calcutta airport for a few hours. I was mostly on my toes to attend to frequent callings and queries from my boss, ready at all times to give the appropriate information and data in a second! In between these rituals, I was listening to the discussions and jokes among the senior colleagues of Secretary rank without actively joining this club! Nevertheless, it was fun and relaxation during the air travel and stay in the Odisha Bhavan, Delhi – away from the daily grind in the State Secretariat! Plan discussion in the Planning Commission was a ritual of higgling and haggling – part of the negotiation was how well you have prepared your case, and the rest is the politics of centre-state relations. The Chief Minister joins at the end to take the negotiation on plan size to a logical conclusion of win-win with the Deputy Chairman of the Planning Commission.

I became familiar with the basics of statistics – the what, whys and hows of rates, ratios, mean and many more jargons. My inborn mathematics phobia notwithstanding, I started applying statistical methods and techniques of evaluation pre, post and concurrent. The familiarity with Census statistics made it easy.Writing position papers, background notes and minutes of review meetings helped me to be precise and specific, and not to beat about the bush and meandering, missing the wood for the trees. I learnt how to construct statistical tables and other forms of presentation of time series data. Computer use was zero then. We were using calculators, and doing manual or mental arithmetical calculations, which we had learnt in school days. When our handwritten reports were getting typed and sometimes printed as booklets, we had a sense of satisfaction and pride. The boss cheered the team with a big 'thank you' and congratulations. Sometimes, he would ask me to get my 'magnum opus'!

Although I was enjoying the work, I was being told that I have not yet been posted as a District Magistrate and Collector, even after a decade of my career, whereas all officers got an independent district charge in seven or eight years on an average.

4

As District Magistrate and Collector and Director of Industries (1975-1979)

On the New Year Day of 1975, I received a Government order of transfer, posting me as District Magistrate and Collector, Puri. Puri district then was one of the thirteen districts of Odisha, with more than five million population, and had four big subdivisions including the State Capital, Bhubaneshwar. Puri – the district headquarter is the Purushottam Kshetra – the Abode of Lord Jagannath – an important 'Dham' of Hindu Sanatan Dharma. The pilgrimage during the annual Car Festival exceeded half a million at that time. There is a flow of pilgrims and tourists from all over the world throughout the year, thanks to the pristine beach, and the beauty of Konark temple.

I had two interesting experiences of the esoteric and mystic kind in the very first month of my joining the new job at Puri. The first was my darshan of Lord Jagannath in His temple soon after I took over charge. I was not very religious in the sense of following rituals. As a child of eleven years, I was brought to Puri by my parents for a delayed sacred thread ceremony in a religious 'Mutt' followed by my walking up to Jagannath temple with the begging bowl as a new 'Brahmachari'. As I entered the temple now after taking charge of the second servant (sevak) of Lord Jagannath (The Maharaja of Puri being the first sevak and District Magistrate as the Vice Chairman of the Temple Management Committee being the second sevak), I had the recollection of the begging bowl I had carried earlier as a child Brahmachari soliciting 'Bhiksha', and I was suddenly transported to a reverie as soon as I was allowed to touch the Holy Feet of Lord Jagannath on the Ratna Singhasan (bejewelled throne). I got an electrifying experience of deep devotional emotion in my body and mind. I wept uncontrollably, and surrendered mentally before the Lord, praying for His constant guidance.

The second mystic experience was my first meeting in January, 1975 with a magnetic personality, who later on ushered me to the path of Shirdi Sai Baba – my Perfect Master, and who has himself spiritually evolved being at the vanguard of the international movement for the spread of SAI faith since the 1990s. This persona by the name of Shri Chandrabhanu Satpathy, who came for darshan of Lord Jagannath, met me along with his father-in-law, Shri Prafulla Chandra Panda – my colleague ADM at Bhubaneshwar then. Shri Satpathy was then a young IPS officer of Uttar Pradesh cadre. In this brief interaction, I could feel something deep within me, which I could not understand at that time. Later events from 1989 onwards did unravel the purport of this mystic encounter in 1975. I would revert to this at the appropriate time.

Life as the head of the district administration is quite tough and exacting. One works almost round the clock, with very little rest. Puri was one of the oldest districts of British India, and the Collector's residence was as old as 1830. Most of these heritage buildings were known as salt offices, as these were being used by East India Company for salt trade prior to the establishment of district headquarters. The bungalow (Collector's residence), situated very close to sea was very airy, but sultry at times. The Governor's summer residence was close by. Governor Ali Akbar Khan used to frequently visit Puri, and grew very fond of me. He would invite me and my wife for lunch or tea at the slightest pretext. If I did not see him for a number of days, he would enquire and even land up in my bungalow during his early morning walk, when I was not up from bed. In some of his public meetings, he would request me to translate his speech into Odia for the audience. He seemed to be very troubled mentally when Emergency was imposed in June 1975, and was awaiting his removal, which happened soon. He was very informal, affable and liberal, and attended the Car Festival of Lord Jagannath with devotion.

I remember an incident during the return car Festival, when we were waiting for 'Pahundi' (carrying of the deities in procession from Gundicha temple to the three Cars) in the enclosed space in two tents – one, where the Governor was waiting, and the other where I was waiting with my wife and children. As I was supervising the arrangement, I could see my Professor of college days (the same professor who had a grudge against me) being pushed and jostled around by the crowd and the police force outside the cordon. I asked the Additional SP, Anadi Sahu, to allow him inside the cordon to my tent, and received him with due respect. He was very keen to be introduced to the Governor, who happened to be the Chancellor of the University, where he was the head of the department of Political Science. The Governor acceded to my request and had a short meeting with him. The Governor asked him: "Are you teaching politics or doing politics?" I thought it was in light humour. But as events unfolded, in a few months, this Professor was removed prematurely from the University on charges of misdemeanour and corruption!

Once the Governor agreed to meet at short notice the famous film star, Vyajantimala, who was visiting Puri. The

Governor's meeting with the film star in my presence was hilarious to say the least. He was elated at the presence of this charming lady; but had forgotten most of what I had told about her films, and was asking humorous questions unrelated to her filmy achievements!

The Chief Minister of Odisha at that time, Mrs. Nandini Satpathy, a firebrand political leader with pro-left Congress caucus, was quite close to the Prime Minister, Indira Gandhi. Just before I joined my Puri post, I called on her at her office in Bhubaneshwar. She asked me if I wanted anything in particular. I did not know what to say. I did not own a car till then (except a ramshackle old ambassador car, which I had bought from a retired bureaucrat, and which was sold off due to high cost of maintenance), and with the motor car advance one got from Government, it was not possible to buy a new car. I mustered courage to request the CM to allow a staff car to be purchased for Collector, Puri (only jeeps were allotted to Collectors then). She was surprised to know that cars are not allotted to Collectors. She telephoned the Finance Secretary, and I became the first District Collector in Odisha to be allotted a car officially! The precedent was followed up, and all Collectors got cars.

Mrs. Satpathy gave me some advice, when I asked for advice – one to be daring and fearless, and to follow your conscience in all your decisions; and second, to think of the poor and the down-trodden in all situations of competing loyalties and claims, subject to the laws of the land. She specifically advised me not to listen to illegal or unreasonable requests, even if these come from political leaders including the CM herself, and not to attend to the CM or Ministers at Puri if I am on my planned tours already (unless I am specifically required for any urgent discussion). I was surprised with the last piece of advice and thought that she perhaps did not mean what she said!

But the events of my tenure as they unfolded proved that she meant what she said and expected Administration to follow this ethos. She never asked me to come and see her at Bhubaneshwar even once during those two years and never sent any unreasonable or out of way request. She was, however, very watchful of the dealings and activities of all District Collectors and seemed to be happy with my performance and dealings vis-à-vis the political leaders and the general public. Even, the proclamation of Emergency did not change her style of governance, except for the list of activities of the opposition political activists, which was coming down from the top through police files to me in connection with detention orders under the draconian Maintenance of Internal Security Act (MISA). The law enforcement relating to unauthorized encroachment of valuable urban land by influential mafia was made very effective and non-interfering, thanks to the discipline during the Emergency days. This was one positive fallout of Emergency apart from the improved work culture and productivity in public offices and factories. The land around the Jagannath temple and sea shore could be restored for public use and gardening following law enforcement, which was not possible earlier. The Chief Minister never interfered, but appreciated it.

One of the retired ICS officers (Nilamani Senapati), who had served as Collector, Puri, 35 years earlier, came to see me at the Collector's residence to express his appreciation of a work, which had remained unfinished in his time. Later in 1979, I was hauled up by the Panda Commission for such 'draconian' measures (Justice Panda, a Vishwa Hindu Parishad loyalist, believed the story of the powerful vested interests) even when the officers had undertaken eviction following due process of law, and I was the appellate authority! Thank God, the State Government after 1980 rejected the Panda Commission report as patently biased and against evidence on record, and our action was justified.

The declaration of national emergency in mid 1975 came as a shock to us in the district administration. Our intelligence source including from police did not present any scenario of unusual activities of subversion or conspiracy in our district, which had the state capital situated within it. I did not find any explanation or justification, except the story that was presented before us from Delhi. We were groping in the dark to catch subverts, saboteurs and enemies of the state. We were compelled to justify the imposition of Emergency. The Head of the State Police assisted by the head of the police intelligence were preparing scene after scene, and creating a 'make believe' world of internal restlessness and threat to security. The district police collected 'appropriate evidence' against the concerned political opponents, and after green signal from above, presented the file with unimpeachable 'evidence' before the District Magistrate. I had no other way to cross-check or vet the evidence. Time was of essence. We were expected to act fast. I delayed a number of cases quite a bit asking for more clinching evidence. This was not to the liking of police top brass and the Government in the Home Department. I could set aside some cases involving minor players. But I had to fall in line in cases involving big players and political leaders.

The political leaders of opposition parties were detained after my orders (with reasoning and justification) were executed by the police. All I could do to mitigate the gravity of the situation was to show due courtesy and consideration to the elderly leaders in terms of better creature comforts in the prisons including more newspapers. A former Chief Minister detenue, Dr. Mahtab, who came on a parole to meet his ailing wife at the Capital Hospital, was received by me. He profusely thanked me for this gesture.

Some of the middle level leaders, who were detained under my orders, thanked me later, as they rose up the ladder in political career to become Ministers. A few politicians prodded me then suggesting that they should be detained.

The judicial board consisting of two High Court Judges confirmed all my orders of detention, after hearing my depositions. There was a perfect synergy in these rather farcical proceedings under the MISA. Government Advocate, Gopal

Ballav Patnaik (who has retired as Chief Justice, Supreme Court) assisted me before the Board.

The first four or six months of Emergency brought in a regime of discipline and higher productivity in work in public offices and institutions – greater punctuality in attendance, no gossip, quicker disposal of files and attending to public grievances. Even the traders, businessman and politicians behaved better. Then happened the re-alignments, mud-slinging, taking of revenge, corruption and favouritism. Planting stories of sabotage became a favourite passion with some. Police became very powerful by manipulating false charges and taking advantage of the situation. We had to be extra alert to avert this phenomenon. It was not easy.

The arrangement for two annual Car Festivals during my tenure was a very hectic affair. As Puri Maharaja was abroad for higher studies in Law, the mantle fell entirely on me. I was, of course, ably assisted by a seasoned temple administrator, Shri Praharaj, who was a good astrologer, and other officials including the SP, Dillip Mahapatra, and Additional SP, Anadi Sahu (who later became an MP). The large number of hereditary Sevaks would come up with their grievances and claims, and sometimes resort to obstructionist tactics like suspending rituals half-way. Such crises arose often; we had to resort to varied strategies (Sam, Dam, Dand, Bhed). The threat of action under Emergency laws was held out as the last resort, and it worked!

The Car Festivals went off smoothly. In one year, the deity, Lord Jagannath refused to climb up the ladder to the Car, despite attempts by the muscular Sevaks carrying Him. I rolled on the ground in front of the Car and wept loudly for all to hear. It worked! Lord Jagannath relaxed His weight and the Sevaks carried Him up the Ladder to His seat inside the Car. Whether one believes it or not, it did work! I believe the Lord of the Universe tested the sincerity and devotion of the mundane devotees. The District Magistrate shed inhibition and ego of his mundane authority and surrendered before the 'Para

Brahm'. This may be a symbolic gesture, but my emotion in prayer was intense and genuine. It gelled in with the collective emotion of lakhs of devotees gathered there. That's how I view this miracle!

Immediately after this incident, I fell ill, had high fever and my legs started swelling. A tantric sevak of Lord Jagannath gave me some special 'prasad' and I became alright. I did not delve into the role of tantra in Jagannath cult.

The DM's bungalow in Puri had a huge compound with many trees, some of which were quite old. My wife had made a swing tied to the branches of an old neem tree for my daughters to play. On a moonlit night during October when I was alone in the house (my wife was visiting her parents with children), I got up hearing the rumblings of strong wind and found an apparition swinging on the dola. I called the security guards, and they also saw someone disappearing in the thick foliage of the compound. I could not understand what it was. A few days later, my staff car driver's daughter, who was playing with my daughters, behaved strangely and started speaking like a British lady (the girl did not know English at all) after she passed through the backyard of our bungalow to go to her house. She appeared to be possessed and became alright after some tantric exorcists treated her! They fixed some iron nails on an old tree, and told me that the wife of a British Collector had committed suicide hundred years back and her ghost still haunts this place! Very difficult to understand such mystic and esoteric phenomena.

The same Neem tree showed symptoms of shapes and figures on its trunk like conch, in 1976 – the year prior to the 'Navakalevar' of the deities Balabhadra, Subhadra and Jagannath – and was short listed as one of a few such trees in the region for final selection of the wood, which will be used for the periodic renewal of the holy statues in Jagannath temple. We were offering worship to the holy Neem tree inside the residential compound. However, this tree was not finally selected!

Many prominent persons with whom I interacted used to visit Puri frequently. I remember Biswanath Dash (ex-Chief Minister, Odisha) and Radhanath Rath (ex-Minister and Editor, *Samaj*) in connection with institutions like Vedic teachings and Satyabadi School of renaissance. The former Principal of Ravenshaw College and D.P.I Dr. Sadasiv Mishra used to visit with me for some State Bank sponsored agricultural projects in Nayagarh area.

Senior officers from State and divisional headquarters were coming to Puri often on official work and for darshan of Lord Jagannath. One senior officer had a very suspicious bent of mind. He would come for inspection; but would leave suddenly, if he suspected that the Chief Minister was likely to come. One night, when this officer arrived, he enquired if the CM was coming. We assured him that there is no programme of the CM; but to his bad luck, the CM decided to come at midnight at a very short notice and next morning, he saw this officer moving in the balcony of the circuit house. When I went to meet the CM in the morning, she enquired about the purpose of the officer's visit. By the time the CM called this officer, he had already left without informing us.

Once V.S. Matthews, Chief Secretary of the State Government, who was very fond of all glamorous things of life and was in the habit of not paying the bills of his stay and boarding, came for a review of my performance in paddy procurement, just three weeks after my joining. He used bullying tactics, like intimidating the subordinate officers and expecting to be provided with the best of food and drinks (scotch whiskey) gratis. My Excise Superintendent came to me before his arrival and told me that he had arranged the drink stuff. I lost my cool and asked him to get lost. The new SP went by the Police Manual and did not arrange a full guard of honour on the ground of non-entitlement. I agreed with the SP. The concerned officer, on arrival in the evening hours, got wild looking at this lackadaisical bandobast, and refused to take tea with minor snacks, like cashew nuts and biscuits, and disposed us in fifteen minutes commenting that paddy procurement was well below the target, and that everything has deteriorated in this district in these three weeks after my joining! He left in a huff, without waiting for dinner. The SP informed me next morning that this officer spent a good part of the evening and night with drinks and gala dinner in a company guest house on the seashore, leaving early in the morning! I do not know how this incident became known to the Chief Minister, who sent her Secretary to find out the details from us.

After the imposition of Emergency, one of the unpleasant actions of the State Administration was the premature compulsory retirement of this senior officer. By some sheer coincidence, I was posted in 1978 by the next Government from my post of Director of Industries to a newly formed Chilka and Maritime Development Corporation as Officer on Special Duty under the same person, who was rehabilitated as Chairman. My transfer got cancelled and I was spared the ordeal of working under this person. I did not bear any grudge, and helped him in his hotel project, when I was Managing Director of IPICOL later.

Balighai beach between Puri and Konark near the estuary of Nuanai river was a serene place of solitude, and I used to spend some time looking at the sandy beach, the waves and the barking deers in the forest. I liked to visit the Ramakrishna Math, Bharat Sevak Samaj, Mother Teresa's Sister of Charity, Atibadi Jagannath Satalahari Math, Guru Nanak's well and one Leprosy Home. I cannot forget the visit of Mother Teresa to the Leprosy Home, where I shared the dais of a meeting with her. Her words, "You must go on giving them love, till it hurts...." are still reverberating in my heart.

The debate we had initiated on the entry of non-Hindus to the Temple of Jagannath remained unresolved, when we were almost coming to a positive decision. Prime Minister Indira Gandhi deferred her visit to the Puri temple (as it became controversial, she having married a non-Hindu) and, instead, visited the Konark temple with her sons and daughters-in-law.

The visit of Union Minister, Jagjivan Ram to the Puri temple went off well and he thanked me profusely for the courtesy shown to him. The CMs of Bihar and West Bengal, Jagannath Mishra and Siddharth Shankar Ray, who came to Puri as well as Jagjivan Ram were kept under watch under orders from Delhi during Emergency.

I recollect the politics of removal of Nandini Satpathy as the CM under orders from Delhi. She had fallen from favour with Indira Gandhi due to Sanjay Gandhi's dislike of her, and the ganging up of some leaders from Orissa against her style of functioning. There was a rumour that that she was conspiring with some CMs of the States of eastern region to revolt against the Central leadership and would resist her removal. A defence plane carrying the Cabinet Secretary, Union Home Secretary and some others landed unannounced at Bhubaneshwar and these officers came to Puri to assess the possible fallout. They discussed with the IG of Police in my presence. I did not come to know all the details, but the CM resigned the next day and President's rule was proclaimed forthwith. This was in early December 1976. In one of the last files, which was cleared by the CM before her resignation, related to a number of transfers in which I figured. I was transferred from Puri and posted at Cuttack as Director of Industries, Odisha, which was a very key job.

The Advisor to Governor, Shri Ramakrishnayya (a former Chief Secretary, Odisha, with whom I had worked in the Planning Department earlier) came to Puri, and told me that my transfer has been cleared in the review of all last orders of the CM, as I was considered non-controversial.

Some of the knotty problems during my Puri days related to the chronic disputes over fishery rights in and around the Chilka Lake, taking over of precious Puri Balukhand Government land from land grabbers, Puri-Konark marine drive, supersession of Puri municipality, defence establishment near Chilka, M.S. Swaminathan's Krishi Vigyan Kendra,

Central Inland Fisheries Institute, initiation of the Sanskrit university project and the first 'Gramin Bank' at Pipli.

I remember taking keen interest in the training of probationary IAS, IFS and OAS officers in my district. Two young ladies, Rajalakshmi (IAS) and Pragna Paramita (IFS) were trained for some period. So also Tarunkanti Mishra (IAS), who retired as the Chief Secretary, Odisha, a few years back. I took good care of them and did not want them to feel isolated and lost, as I had experienced in my days as Assistant Collector. I used to encourage them to accompany me in some tours in the district. I hope, they did not find me overbearing. One OAS trainee, Gopinath Mohanty, had eloped with his girlfriend to take my blessing for their marriage, which took place at Puri, much to the chagrin of the girl's parents, who complained to my Revenue Divisional Commissioner, Nalinikant Panda. Gopinath has retired as an IAS officer, and his wife, Sanchita is a political leader in the BJP, and became an MLA.

I remember my friend from Allahabad University days, Ramjilal Patwari, who qualified to join the Central Civil Services with us in 1964 (but was not taken due to a police record against him, as a student union leader in Allahabad), was practising in Puri bar, but was more engaged in politics and family business. We used to meet off and on, and he was very unbiased in his advice on public affairs during my Puri days. Ramji died a premature death after a surgery in 1990, a few days before my wife's death. We used to together attend spiritual discourses in Puri, whenever I was free.

My Director of Industries Days at Cuttack (December 1976-May 1979)

After leaving Puri, towards the end of December 1976, I joined the 'glamorous' post of Director of Industries, Odisha and continued there till May 1979. I occupied a Government bungalow constructed on a high ground inside the historical 'Barabati Fort', which was the seat of power of Odisha kings and later of the British Raj. It overlooked the Mahanadi river and a moat. The fort contained a very ancient Gad-Chandi temple and Cuttack Club. Some people believed that the goddess 'Chandi' goes on a trip to the ancient Shiva temple on the bank of Mahanadi on some nights, when the sound of the divine anklets could be heard. Some of my family relatives had told me that they heard such sound in the aangan of the bungalow where I lived. Quite difficult to believe!

Two successive Governments were in power during this two and a half years period – a Congress Party government for a short period with Kanhucharan Lenka (my classmate of college days) as Minister, Industries, followed by a Janata Party government with Nilamani Routray as the CM and Harish Chandra Baxipatra as the Minister, Industries. Baxipatra was a leader of Student's Federation (leftist organization) in college days, when I had joined as a member of this group in school. He was close to Biju Patnaik, who was then the Union Steel Minister.

My equation with the Ministers was good. I was lucky to report to a seasoned bureaucrat, R.N. Das (1959 batch of IAS), who worked as Secretary, Industries Department during this period. He was very pragmatic and clear headed and prompt in taking decisions. He was very supportive and positive in his supervision and guidance. Two of my colleagues, D.C. Gupta, succeeded by Samar Mahapatra ably assisted as Additional Director. Both D.C. Gupta and Samar Mahapatra having retired as Government of India Secretaries, now live in Noida and Dwaraka (Delhi), respectively.

The association of industries had very frank interaction with me from time to time on their common problems, and I tried to attend to their genuine and reasonable needs. Ancillary industrial estates development around major industries was our priority. So also was bank financing issues for small and tiny industries. We activated the co-ordination committees, project review forum and one-stop clearances, particularly with Orissa State Financial Corporation and Orissa Small Industries Corporation.

We welcomed the initiative of Union Industry Minister, George Fernandes, on District Industry Centres, and were the first state to open such centres in all districts at one go. Such centres became the hive of activities. We got some dynamic young IAS officers and Bank officers to lead these centres, along with other technical experts from the cadre of State Industries Service. The promotional avenues opened up in leaps and bounds for experienced and meritorious officers. The experiment was worth it in terms of its spin effects. Many small, tiny and village industries sprang up. The State Finance Corporation, Small Industries Corporation and Industrial Promotion and Investment Corporation became quite pro-active.

The handicraft, cottage and village industries were given special attention. The cooperative corporations and societies started looking up. Linkage was established with raw materials, technology, marketing and export. We studied the industrial promotion in Maharashtra and Gujarat, and started adopting some promising practices from there.

I used to attend the national licensing committee meetings to get expeditious clearance for some major or medium industries in Odisha, Shri U.C. Aggarwal, a senior officer of Odisha cadre, who was Chairman, Industrial Development Corporation, had attended one such meeting with me to plead for a letter of intent for a new unit. He was a very fine officer and highly respected in the Government of India, having worked as Establishment Officer, and later as Personnel Secretary. He preferred to sit on the back bench reserved for parties to industrial license and asked me to sit on the main table representing the State Government. The Committee Chair noticed this and requested him to come to the main table. Shri Aggarwal continued his interest in public administration after retirement and was associated actively as Editor of the Journal of Public Administration.

As Director of Industries, I was vested with the power of regulating and controlling some scarce raw materials for industrial use. One such material was in short supply and was being sold in black market by some industrial units. We were making surprise raids. In one such raid, an industrial unit, which had the partnership of a young entrepreneur, who happened to be the son of a prominent political leader, was caught doing black marketing. I got a telephonic call from Sri Biswal, Secretary to Chief Minister Nilamani Routray, requesting me to withdraw the case, to which I politely declined. The very next day, I was served with a transfer order posting me to a non-descript job of Officer-on-Special Duty in a newly formed Chilka Development Corporation under the Chairmanship of a person, who was compulsorily retired by the earlier Government. The Additional Director of Industries, Samar Mahapatra was ordered to take over as Director of Industries.

I got ready to hand over charge forthwith. But the Industries Secretary (R.N. Das), knowing the reason of my sudden transfer, took it up with the Minister, who instructed him from Chennai (where he was on tour) that in no case I should hand over charge until his return and further instruction. The Minister took up the issue with the C.M. and held out a subtle threat to the CM that he would expose the scandal, unless my transfer order was cancelled. I received the order of cancellation and continued in the job. But I resolved mentally to go on a deputation to the Government of India.

In another instance of a raid on a small scale industrial unit in Sundergarh district where similar misuse and black marketing of imported raw material was unearthed, a young entrepreneur of the unit (from a traditional trading family) dared to approach my wife with costly gifts, which were declined by her; but he later came to me in my office and handed over an envelope purportedly with a representation letter. As I opened the envelope, I found bundles of currency notes instead of his representation. I lost my cool, detained him and informed the IG of Vigilance, (Shri Padhy), who came personally, and advised me not to press it further with criminal case, but gave a pep talk on ethics to the young entrepreneur. We, however, went ahead with prosecution in this case.

My colleagues in related organizations of the Government, like Small Industries Service Institute (SISI), Government of India, Directorate of Export Promotion and Marketing, Orissa State Finance Corporation, Orissa Small Industries Corporation were very cooperative and supportive of my efforts and vice versa. We worked with perfect synergy and understanding and went on joint tours sometimes. I enjoyed working with them. I remember D.P. Bhattacharya and Ashok Mahapatra (he has retired as a Secretary in the Government of India) in S.I.S.I., Abhaya Rath (Director, EPM), Sunil Patnaik (he has resigned from IAS and is Swami Nirliptanand now) and G.C. Patra in OSFC.

The Development Commissioner, Small Scale Industries, Government of India, liked our work on formation and operationalization of District Industries Centre, and hinted the possibility of me going to Delhi as his colleague. I was getting an offer of posting as the Resident Director of India Investment Centre abroad. There was also a nomination for me to go as Advisor, Planning to the Government of Afghanistan under the ITEC programme. I was, however, not in a position to accept any of these offers due to the exigency of my family responsibility heightened with my father's indifferent health in 1979 (He expired in September that year). I looked for a posting related to Government of India deputation in Odisha, if it was possible. The job which came my way soon was the Director of Census Operations for Odisha under the Census Commissioner, Government of India. Shri Bibhuti Tripathy, the former Census Director, Orissa, of 1971 Census called me one day and sought my consent before his recommendation to Shri P. Padmanabha, the Census Commissioner of India for 1981 Census. Recollecting fondly the work of District Census Officer in 1971 Census, I readily agreed. Thus came my first Government of India deputation in May, 1979, ending my lingering discomfiture with the State Government.

5

Getting Entrenched in Census and Population Studies (1979-83)

The new found freedom from the glamour of Industries Directorate was so welcoming and thrilling! Others thought of this change as 'retrograde' in terms of career building. To many career administrative service officers, Census work looked dull, drab and an aberration from glamorous and attractive jobs in Industry, Commerce and economic ministries. One senior colleague, R. Srinivasan, who was my neighbour at Cuttack, advised me to wriggle out of this posting. It is coincidental that he was the Additional Secretary, Department of Justice in Home Ministry, and was instrumental in my appointment as the Registrar General and Census Commissioner, India, in 1989.

Apart from organising the gigantic time bound synchronous administrative and statistical exercise of the 1981 housing, population and economic Census with the help of personnel, who are not under your direct control, the job involves quite a bit of scholarly intellectual work in the preparation of analytical reports, of which one has to take the authorship. The ICS officer, Ashok Mitra, the legendary Census Commissioner of 1961 Indian Census, used to refer to the Census Directors as "Scholar Administrators". I took pride in my job and worked hard to activate the mechanism of Census taking in Odisha.

The State Census Directorate office was housed in two rented buildings at Cuttack when I joined in May, 1979. By 1981, the new building of its own was ready in Bhubaneshwar and the office was shifted there. Most of the staff was commuting from Cuttack for some time until the staff quarters were built in Bhubaneshwar. The preparatory work for the 1981 Census taking in Odisha kept me very busy. Instruction circulars were being sent to Census Officers at district and sub-district levels at regular intervals; training of master trainers were held at state and district levels; and the cascading training at sub-district centres was held right down to Block headquarters and village clusters. I made extensive whirl-wind tours of all districts repeatedly between 1979 and 1981. After the main Census operations, the work of tabulation of data at regional make-shift offices and data entry and processing centre at Bhubaneshwar made headway as per schedule. The Census Director's conferences convened by my boss, Census Commissioner, India, P. Padmanabha, at different places, like Delhi, Goa, Mysore and Nainital were very lively and refreshing. Mr. Padmanabha was an excellent person to work with. He was the 12th Census Commissioner in the chain of India's Census taking beginning in 1971-72, and the fourth after Independence. I missed meeting the 1951 Census Commissioner, R. A. Gopalaswamy due to his death in 1989. I had very close interaction with the 1961 Census Commissioner, Ashok Mitra, in the 1980s and 1990s and also with the 1971 Census Commissioner, Chandrasekhar, who had visited my district, when I was the District Census Officer. Little did I know then that I would join this chain as the 1991

Census Commissioner of India. My successor – the 2001 Census Commissioner, J.K. Banthia (who recently retired as the Chief Secretary, Maharashtra) and the 2011 Census Commissioner, C. Chandramouli, have involved me in advisory capacity.

After the major part of Census taking, data tabulation and report writing was over, I was nominated along with Bihar Census Director, Bipin Behari Lal (My IAS batch mate and close friend) for a year's post-graduate study of population at the David Owen Centre of Population Growth Studies at the University of Wales College of Cardiff, UK in September, 1982. Some students in their mid-service career joined us from China, Bangladesh, UK, West Indies and African countries of Uganda and Madagascar. Coming back to student days at this age in life was a challenge. Preparing our own food, attending long hours in library, computer and communication labs, and the discipline of learning demography and population programmes were very exacting, but proved to be useful for my future career. The inter-disciplinary syllabus on population study, along with the exposure to country case studies on population scenarios, policies and programmes made me look at demography from a more human rights and gender lense. The Director of the Centre, Casper Brook, coined a new word for the study, 'Demology'. We were given opportunity to attend important seminars and conferences at Oxford University, London School of Economics and Political Science, and the Welsh School of Medicine. We got over the initial disadvantage of lack of academic background in statistics and the bureaucratic dependence on stenographers and Personal Assistants. I liked interaction with teachers like Neil Thomas (a Marxist economist and demographer) Jack Liggett, Tom Gabriel, David Owen, Jack Parsons, and students like John Worley, B.B. Lal and Li Ai Wei. During my trip to the UK in October, 2013, I was invited by John Worley to his house in Haddenham village in Buckinghamshire where I met Prof. Neil Thomas and shared our thoughts on population.

The wet and cold weather of UK notwithstanding, I enjoyed my stay there; visited many places in UK, Europe, USA and Canada on holiday breaks. I met my two younger sisters (Charu and Reeta) and their families in Montreal and New York and my niece (Minati) and her husband, Sarat Prahraj (Space Scientist) at Huntsville, Alabama. I also met my old college friend, Digambar Mishra (who is now Dean of Miles College of Birmingham). I met Rajendra Das at Dusseldorf, Germany, a couple of times. He was working in Mannesmann Demag, and was my contemporary in Ravenshaw College. I was frequently visiting my first cousin, Dr. Lalit Mohan Mahapatra, an ENT surgeon, settled at a huge farm house near Basingstoke Hospital about 40 miles south of London. He had married a British lady, who was very hospitable and affectionate. Both of them are no more.

My seminar papers and thesis on rural development and population policy in India were well appreciated by the faculty and examiners. Dr. Malcolm Potts, the well known population and family planning expert from USA, was my external examiner and Neil Thomas was my supervisor. Little did I know that one day I would be part of the international advisory committee with Malcolm Potts, and that I would be part of the architecture of Indian's first comprehensive National Population Policy, 2000.

My dear friend from 1964 Mussoorie days, K.B. Verma (who left us for heavenly abode in October, 2012) had warned me that I have to beat the cold of UK either in the 'rug' way or the 'rum' way. I was a teetotaller until I was advised by Director, Caspar, to take a little whiskey as a pain killer for my toothache. Treatment and extraction of tooth in Britain was very expensive (not covered in our health insurance) as also the hair-cuts. I deferred both, growing long hippie-like hair, and getting habituated to sip Teacher's Scotch whiskey, whenever I had toothache. I developed a liking for Scotch whiskey and did not mind taking a social drink once in a while till 1989, after which I reverted to my earlier status of a teetotaller! I thereafter, substituted Scotch whisky with good quality 'Darjeeling' tea, which gives me the aroma and flavour similar to Scotch whisky, but definitely less harmful. I was never a smoker. Thrice in life, I have tasted 'Bhang' without my knowledge – once as a 'laddoo' given to me by a friend at Bhubaneshwar; once as the Prasad of Lord Jagannath during Snan Purnima at Puri, and once during 'Holi' celebration in Delhi in 1990. I behaved very abnormally on all these occasions. I think such intoxicants did not suit me at all. I now get the intoxication of devotional love, to which none of the earlier intoxicants matched in terms of abiding bliss. Not even the intoxication of romantic worldly love.

While at Cardiff, some of us took a Sunday trip in winter to a beautiful Welsh Coast south of Swansea, and walked into a dry stony creek inside the sea to climb up a hill island. A little later, we realised that the hill was surrounded by sea water all around, which came swirling due to high tide, and we were cut off from the main land. We had no way to communicate (there was no cell phone then). However, one member of our team, John Worley, who was left with the car in the main land, realised the gravity of the situation and approached the coast guards, who commissioned a Royal Air Force helicopter rescue just before nightfall and development of nasty windy weather. There was no shelter in that hill island, and we would have frozen to death at night! The coast guard chided us for not heeding their warning on the notice board (which was written in Welsh language). The rescue operation was televised and we became known for our misadventure! I ruminated over this incident recently (October, 2013) when I met Neil Thomas and John Worley of Cardiff days in England.

During my Cuttack days (Industry Director and Census Director), I had become a member of the Rotary Club of Cuttack, proposed by Anang Patnaik (who retired as a Judge in the Supreme Court). I used to attend Rotary meetings at places where I was travelling in the course of my official trips. I did attend some meetings in Cardiff too. Club membership in an international movement like Rotary gave an opportunity for wider socialization and social service. I could not, however, continue the membership beyond a few years.

I took interest in classical music and ghazals while I was at Cuttack from 1979 and continued this interest when I came to Bhubaneshwar in 1981. I became an active member of Bhubaneshwar Music Circle pioneered by Sardar Santok Singh, and was elected to remain as President of the Circle for some time. Some of the music lovers of the time at Cuttack and Bhubaneshwar Music Circle were Mahendra Mishra, Daud Rahman, Sudhansu Kumar Mishra (who is no more), Sarat Satpathy, Badal Sen (who is no more) Japani Babu, Dhiren Ray, Shantanu Mahapatra and Durga Prasanna Mishra. They were very active members and organisers of the music circles at Bhubaneshwar and Cuttack.

We invited many illustrious singers and musicians like Talat Muhammad, Ghulam Mustafa, Sajjan-Rajan Mishra, Girija Devi, V.G. Jog, Hari Chaurasia, Singh brothers, Parveen Sultana, Rashid Khan, Amzad Ali Khan and organised annual sangeet sammelans with sponsored artists of fame. We spotted a few budding talents like Rashmi and Radhika from Delhi and arranged their performance. The ghazals made our heart yearn for love and the anguish of separation from the beloved, and the classical music elevated our soul to lofty heights of spiritual reflection. Begum Akhtar and Mehndi Hassan were my favourite ghazal singers. My interest in such music waned after 1990.

My earlier foray into music has been intermittent since childhood. My elder sister, Premanani was my first mentor in childhood! In my adolescent days in Ravenshaw College, I was associated briefly with a radio artist on a platonic romantic level. I became a part of a music circle in Allahabad under the direction of Bidhu Samant. Thereafter, I was part of group songs sung at Mussoorie with expert singers like R.P. Sinha (My IAS batch mate) in the lead. At Nagpur ITO Training College, I learnt to sing Bengali, Odia and Hindi songs along with some other colleagues, led by Asim Roychaudhury and also learnt guitar for a while. I remember our singing the Rabindra Sangeet "Mano moromeghera Sange"…. (My mind floats with the monsoon clouds) in All India Radio, Nagpur in 1965. I, however, did not pursue my interest seriously, as I became a part of the 'steel-frame' administrative service, except occasional forays with some organisational role or patronization, like in Cuttack and Bhubaneshwar music circles. Over last two decades, my interest has been limited to devotional music – SAI bhajans and prayer songs (Artis) in particular, and a bit of serious classical music. The soul-stirring songs written by C.B. Satpathy are very appealing.

From the romantic songs in the late 1950s, 60s and 70s to the songs of agony of separation in the early 90s, to the soulful songs of divine Love from 2000 onwards – all reflect the emotional 'bhava' of human (man-woman) relationship sublimated to God-Guru-Devotee relationship. Each one has its own charm in certain stage of life's journey. You look back, ruminate and introspect. I still like to hum some old nostalgic numbers when the old mood of yesteryears sets in. A sample of some numbers (first line), which have been embedded in mind, is presented below:

Phase I

Kaun aya mere man ke dware
(Who has come to the door of my mind)

Ab jaane ki zid na karo
(Please do not insist on parting now)

Jalte hein jiske liye
(For whom the lamp of your eyes light up)

Jindagi ussi ki hai, jo kissi ka ho gaya
(Life is only for one, who belongs to someone else in emotive love)

Phase II

Ulfata ki nayee manzil ko chala
(The goal of affection has changed)

Waqt ne kiya, kya hasi sitam
(what a beautiful injustice time has done)

Tum na jaane kis jahaan me kho gaye
(I don't know in which world you have got lost)

Phase III

Pritam Aan Milo.......
(Come my Beloved to meet)

Tu Pyaar ka Sagar hai
(You are the Ocean of love)

E Malik tere bande hum
(O Lord, we are your servants)

Allah tero naam, Ishwar tero naam
(O God, your name is Allah, your name is Ishwar)

The last four songs are now perceived as addressed to God with devotion and are more appealing compared to earlier ones, though those had appealed to me in the past quite intensely.

6

Senior Positions in State Government (1983-1989)

Revenue Divisional Commissioner, Central Division

On return from study abroad in August, 1983, I was reverted from Central deputation back to the State Government of Odisha, and was posted on promotion to super-time scale as Revenue Divisional Commissioner, Central Division, with headquarters at Cuttack. This Division consisted of four big districts of Cuttack, Puri, Baleshwar and Mayurbhanj, and I had to discharge the supervisory and appellate/reviewing duties under a statute. There were three Divisions in the State. Divisional Commissioners were, according to the protocol, the senior most officers in the hierarchy next to Member, Board of Revenue and Chief Secretary. With the Secretaries to Government being upgraded to similar or higher rank in the last 50 years, the importance of this post had already come down, though according to the protocol, they continued to enjoy a higher rank.

I was taking over charge from a very senior officer (of 1957 IAS batch), Ramakanta Mishra, who had the reputation for simplicity, honesty and goodness with the least ego. He shared his experience and 'pearl' circulars of wisdom, which were of great use to me in my work.

The RDC bungalow had a huge compound with a pond, an orchard and bushes and foliage all around. There was a perch in the middle of the pond as a resting place for birds. A residential office was attached to the residence, which had a window air-conditioner, which was useful in summer to provide comfort even to the nearby bedroom. The RDC had ceremonial roles on Independence and Republic days, and was entitled to full 'guard of honour' in all official trips within the Division.

The main office and the Court of the RDC was a few kms away near the High Court and Board of Revenue on one side, and Ravenshaw Collegiate School (which was my alma mater for two years) on the other. I used to assiduously attend to my Court work at least twice a week, and disposed off revenue and other statutory appeals and revisions to the best of my judgement. The reading of case laws and judgements of higher courts made me somewhat knowledgeable of the judicial interpretations of laws. Many senior advocates (some of them have been elevated to the High Court and Supreme Court) were appearing in my Court and enlightened me with their legal acumen, knowledge and insight. Justice Deepak Mishra of the Supreme Court, was an advocate, who assiduously prepared and argued cases in my Court.

Review, inspection and coordination of the work of district administration took most of my time. Apart from annual inspections of the four offices of district collectors and a sample of sub-divisional and Tahsil officers, I had to inspect some special projects, like Salandi Command Area Development and the tiger and elephant reserves. I also remained in additional charge of two other Divisions (Sambalpur and Berhampur) for a few months, which took me to undertake visits to those areas.

My tenure of one and a half years was more or less smooth, except for one or two incidents of law and order at Paradeep Port and the murder of a police officer. I was visiting the sub-divisional headquarters of Jagatsinghpur with Collector, Cuttack, when we got information of this incident, and I proceeded to Paradeep along with the Collector. The police reprisal was obstructed, but the entire issue was politicised. Since I was present at the spot, I could not be the authority to enquire; it was entrusted to Additional Chief Secretary. In retrospect, I felt that I should not have been over-zealous to go there. Such wrong judgements happen. I was critical of a senior Minister, Basant Biswal, who was interfering in the election process in his constituency. The SDO was behaving in a manner as if he was at the Minister's beck and call. I chided and cautioned the officials through the Collector, Cuttack, which was not to the liking of the Minister. I was suddenly transferred to Bhubaneshwar as Managing Director, Industrial Promotion and Investment Corporation in January, 1985, as a sequel.

Managing Director, Industrial Promotion and Investment Corporation Limited (IPICOL)

My stint in IPICOL lasted for only four months. With my earlier experience as Director of Industries, it did not take much time to settle down in my job. I had to keep my family in a small government quarter at Cuttack, so that my children's education in the mid year would not suffer. My predecessor-in-office, Vivek Pattanayak had worked very hard to promote new industries and hotel projects, and I had to come up to the expectations of the entrepreneurs. I was lucky to have a number of knowledgeable colleagues including a Chairman, in J.K. Bhattacharya (1959 batch IAS), who gave me full support and guidance. We tried to expedite investment decisions in tandem with the all-India financial institutions, like IDBI, IFCI and ICICI.

Secretary to Chief Minister, Odisha

I received an order of transfer posting me as 'Secretary to Chief Minister, which came to me both as a surprise and dismay. I was not much known to the CM, J.B. Patnaik (I had met him a couple of times during his visit to Puri as Union Minister, and at Bhubaneshwar when I was the RDC). Quite likely, my batch mate and friend Sudhansu Mishra, who had been working as Secretary to the CM for five years, might have suggested my name.

I was very apprehensive that the work of CM's Secretariat will not suit me. I met the Chief Secretary, Gian Chand and wanted to wriggle out of this posting. I was advised not to take this move. So I joined the so-called 'powerful' post. My colleagues in service, the Ministers and political leaders congratulated me and started looking at me very reverentially.

I could not survive in this job for more than one and half years. Working from 9 a.m. to midnight daily (including Saturdays and Sundays); attending to Cabinet meetings (preparing briefs and comments on notes, and press notes for the CM after the decisions), preparing briefs for all CM's officials meetings in the State and Delhi, making suggestions and comments on all official files put up to the CM, briefs on policy formulations, transfer and postings of senior officers kept me awfully busy. I used to have regular interaction with Secretaries, Chief Secretary, and sometime Ministers to understand their viewpoints before placing considered comments to the CM for his final decisions.

The mischief value of this post was great indeed! I tried my best to do as less damage as possible, and kept my personal biases and impressions aside. Sharing the power with the CM is like the snake's venom – it gets into your head, and you become prone to haughtiness and impetuousness. In the eyes of the public, you are the most powerful bureaucrat! They expect you to attend to their grievances on behalf of the CM J.B. Patnaik was a shrewd politician and seasoned administrator. He would go to any length to keep his political control intact. He had many sources of knowledge about men and events. I was very careful while giving feedback and opinions, even if it might not be to his liking. He used to work for long hours in his office, and had political discussions interspersed with official work. The review meetings of projects or programmes were being held invariably in evenings, going up to 11 p.m. For the first few days, I was dozing off in some late evening meetings, but one gets used to this routine.

The CM used to come to the office after his morning meetings at his residence around 11.30 a.m. and would break for lunch at 3 p.m. or so. He would come again at 5 p.m. and leave office around midnight. His secretariat would, however, work from 9 a.m. to past midnight. Cups after cups of tea would keep us awake and alert!

When I am not meeting the CM, my time was spent going through the files and preparing briefs after discussion with my colleagues in the Secretariat. I was lucky to have a colleague, Deputy Secretary in Madan Panda, who had read the files thoroughly, and discussed with me the implications and ramifications of important issues along with the tricky legal and constitutional matters. Additional Secretary, Harmohan Patnaik was also very helpful. Harmohan met with untimely death in 1990. L.C. Amarnathan, an IPS Officer in CM office was a tower of strength.

As the files were piling up with the CM not giving us time due to his other engagements, we would muster courage and request him for a special one day retreat for exclusive file clearance at Nandan Kanan zoo guest house on a holiday. The CM was not disturbed by other works or phone calls. He would carefully go through all important files and papers, even my briefing and write his decisions then. He developed confidence in us, but would not trust us fully. That was his nature. In the case of some of the files with tricky political implications, he would postpone decision to an appropriate time.

J.B. Patnaik knew how to write his own speech, even when we would come up with a draft. His editorial experience in newspaper and writing skill stood him in good stead. He was very learned in Sanskrit language, and had a big personal library with rare books. During his Delhi trips, he would visit book shops in Daryaganj area and spend time with us to buy books.

He had developed very good rapport with Indira Gandhi, and after her, with Rajiv Gandhi, though he had initial problem in winning his confidence. The news of starvation deaths, migration and sale of children in Kalahandi made big headlines in national newspapers and magazines like *India Today*. Officers from the PMO started making derogatory remarks in their telephone calls and letters to me. I helped in putting a report together, explaining the situation and the CM sent a letter to the PM Rajiv Gandhi's visit to Kalahandi was being projected to put the CM on a spot, but J.B. Patnaik managed it very dexterously to his advantage, and his critics and opponents were proved wrong. Later, some stories that exposed his alleged immoral activities appeared in the *Illustrated Weekly*, which cast a shadow on his image. His most intimate cabinet colleague, Basant Biswal, became his critic, and things started looking bad for him. He was giving less time for review meetings. He went for a reshuffle of portfolios and induction of new Ministers in his Cabinet. He was feeling quite lonely at that time and consulted me and Madan Panda, (Deputy Secretary) on the above issues. He filed defamation suits with very high stakes, and the 'Weekly' had to come down with an apology.

I was not getting involved in any of the political stratagem or anything remotely related to that. My role was limited strictly to official business in the CM's office.

Secretary to the State Government, Mining and Geology Department

Towards the end of 1986, I was served with a transfer order posting me as Secretary, Mining and Geology Department, along with the Chairmanship of the Orissa Mining Corporation and OMC Alloys Ltd. Mining was a very small department, but was very critical and sensitive in view of the existence of major reserves of valuable minerals in the state and the need for their rational and balanced exploitation.

The Minister of State, Mining, Mohan Nag, was a God fearing and honest person, and I had no problem in advising him. Two of my colleagues, Joint Secretary (Rai Charan Das) and Deputy Secretary (Sura Prasad Das) worked with sincerity and honesty, and I spent the next two years and three months with a clear conscience and without fear or favour. The only problem we faced was from a senior supervisory officer (Chief Secretary), who would sit over our files for days and send back with silly and unnecessary queries a couple of times, instead of calling us for discussion. For reasons best known to him, he would dilly-dally and put the blame at our door, when complaint of red-tape came to the notice of the CM. This ended in an unpleasant confrontation, which exposed him! He was unhappy that his indiscriminate guest entertainment at the expense of OMC. was put to a stop, when I was the Chairman. He wrote an indifferent assessment report on my performance as the Reporting Officer, which was completely superseded by the Minister and the CM, giving me 'Outstanding' report with detailed justification, as I came to know later. Thank God, I got my two promotions (Additional Secretary and Secretary, Government of India) without any hitch on time. I had very high regards for Chief Secretary N.K. Panda, and hold no malice against him.

During my tenure, I had the chance to visit Japan for negotiations on the sale of OMC's chromite and charge chrome (OMC Alloys) to steel manufactures in Japan. The negotiations were very tough. We had regular discussion with MMTC on the export of iron and manganese ore. The manufacture of charge chrome in OMC Alloy's factory had started; but there were technical snags in the technology transfer from foreign firms. We were intensely engaged in smoothing it out.

The renewal of mining lease for the chromite mines came up in my time. The private players wanted a bigger cake. The matter went up to the Government of India, and the Union Mines Secretary, Mr. Rao took up the hearing very astutely. We prepared our case in great detail, and I personally appeared in the hearings with strong arguments in favour of the public sector, OMC.

For a few months, I remained in additional charge of Housing and Urban Development Department including the Chairmanship of State Housing Board. I held interactions with the Government of India, HUDCO and the National Commission on Urbanization during this period.

I was a Board member (representing the State Government) in the South-Eastern Coal Field Ltd., a Government of India subsidiary of Coal India headquartered at Bilaspur. Our efforts to open a separate company for Odisha coal fields paid dividends and Mahanadi Coal Field Ltd. of Coal India started with headquarters at Sambalpur.

7

Senior Administrative Positions in Central and State Governments (1989-2002)

Registrar General and Census Commissioner, India

In mid 1989, I was transferred and posted in New Delhi on Government of India deputation as Registrar General and Census Commissioner, India. My posting order was delayed due to a controversial claim to this job by Indian Statistical Service officers, supported by some academics like Ashish Bose in the wake of some tiff with my predecessor, Mr. Vijay Verma. They took up the issue with the Prime Minister and my posting file went into hibernation for almost a year. The Home Ministry's Additional Secretary, Mr. R. Srinivasan consulted me and Mr. Padmanabha, the 1981 Census Commissioner, and prepared a strong case for an IAS officer experienced in Census taking to be on this job, and finally the Prime Minister agreed to my posting. Prof. Ashish Bose later wrote in a book on 1991 Census vindicating the suitability of only IAS officers for this job.

Since I joined quite late for the 1991 Census, I had to act swiftly to make up for the lost time. Working for long hours and rushing from one state to another, I was able to fill up the key posts of Census Director and Deputy Directors. Getting additional posts sanctioned from Finance Ministry and their recruitment and updating the preparatory work for 1990 House listing operation were tough jobs. The Home Secretaries of my time, who were very supportive of my work, were Kalyana Krishnan, Shiromani Sharma, Madhav Godbole and N.N. Vohra. So also were my two senior colleagues, R. Srinivasan and Arun Sinha (both are no more) from the Department of Justice.

Taking the people into confidence, we could get Census conducted in Assam after two decades. The Census could not be conducted in Jammu and Kashmir due to unusual situation developing from 1989 onwards. One of our Census office buildings was attacked and bombed, when I planned a visit there. We prepared estimated projected statistics for J&K State based on 1981 census and the mini-Census of 1987. The Prime Minister, Chandrasekhar, took keen interest in the Census work and wrote to all Chief Ministers. Later, the Union Home Minister, S.B. Chavan, gave full back up to us. Most of the Home Secretaries during my tenure were very supportive of the Census Commissioner's work, and commended my performance in many ways. Within a fortnight of the end of Census taking, the provisional data were released by me in a huge Press Conference attended by national and international media. India's Census appeared on the international map with a lot of publicity. The *Time* magazine carried a big article. Some of the colleagues in the RGI office, who ably assisted me in my work are K.S. Natarajan, Rama Rao, H.P. Sharma, O.P. Sharma, as well as the State Directors of Census, like J.K. Banthia, R.P. Singh, R.N. Senapati and others.

I became a founding member of the International Association of Census Directors established at East-West Centre, Honolulu (USA) and was invited to present India's Census story in many fora in the USA, Japan, South Korea and China. Some of my colleagues were invited to extend technical assistance in some countries in Africa and Asia.

We processed the voluminous data with appropriate edit, coding and cleansing, and got all main tabulations completed in next two years or so. Reports on important profiles of housing and population were prepared and published, receiving wide acclaim nationally and internationally. We had an open door policy to cater to the needs of data users. We announced a policy for limited availability of edited raw data to data users from the research community. We planned for the revival of micro research studies of socio-anthropological type (like village studies and SC/ST studies) undertaken after 1961 and 1971 Census. It is, however, a different story that these decisions were not implemented after I left the Census organisation at the end of 1994. More detailed information on languages (like 1961 Census) was planned in tabulation.

I was co-opted as an ex-officio member of the Executive Committee of the Indian Association for the Study of Population (IASP) during 1990-1994. Later on, I was taken as a life member of IASP and a member of the Board of Trustees, which I continue to discharge even now. This association of population scientists and demographers has honoured me to deliver George Simmons Memorial Lecture during their annual conference at Annamalai in 2004 and with a life-time achievement award in 2010 at the Bhubaneshwar conference.

I was nominated by the Government of India as a member of the official delegation to the International Conference on Population and Development at Cairo in September, 1994. ICPD 1994 was a major watershed in the history of looking at population issues from a rights-based and gender-sensitive angle. The progressive and secular forces, as well as the voices of women's groups triumphed over the regressive, fundamentalist, conservative and diehard population control groups in a major way in this historic meeting. I had the pleasure of participating and being part of this historic transition process leading to ideas of sexual and reproductive health and rights, along with gender equity and equality, women's empowerment and population development nexus in a non-demographic perspective.

The learnings at the Cardiff centre in the 1980s got further re-enforced for me in ICPD, 1994, and I re-interpreted the Census statistics from this new perspective. All this helped me to come out of the authoritarian bureaucratic 'population control' and stand alone target driven family planning strategy mind-set into a holistic rights based and gender sensitive Reproductive Health and Rights mind-set, situated within the paradigm of 'Population and Development'. With the firm conviction and knowledge of pro-poor, pro-women and pro-people approach, I could convince the right wing conservative BJP led coalition government to approve the new National Population Policy in 2000, when I worked as the Secretary to the Government of India in Health and Family Welfare Ministry. I could get broad consensus across all political parties and the civil society including the women's groups.

One of the break-throughs during the 1991 Census was the last minute modification of the questionnaire and the instructions to enumerators to elicit better response for women's work or economic activity, which was being withheld or concealed in earlier censuses. Women were generally perceived as housewives, and all their work in agriculture, household industry and allied occupation was not being elicited with searching questions due to male bias and patriarchal society. The women's groups, SNDT Women's university and UNIFEM had failed to convince my predecessor (V.S. Verma), but took it up again after my joining in 1989. I was convinced of the need for retrieving the women's work status, and took a belated decision when the Census questionnaire and instruction booklets were about to be notified and printed. The results of the 1991 Census showed that our initiative worked, though the real dividend came in the next two (2001 and 2011) Censuses. The women's groups and feminists appreciated our gesture, and I was elected as a life member of the Centre for Women's Development Studies (CWDS) a few years later. There are very few male members in the CWDS, which is an invincible bastion of feminists in India. A vivid account of our belated, but timely initiative has been given in a book written by Madhubala Nath of UNIFEM (She is the Country Director of Engender Health now).

Following the Mandal Commission report and related agitation, there was a move to include caste enumeration in the 1991 Census, which was opposed by me on the ground of non-feasibility at short notice, and also the apprehension of Census getting biased and politicised. Even after the Census was over (without caste enumeration), some political leaders like the then CM of Bihar, Lalu Yadav, tried to persuade me to permit the use of individual schedules, to go back and collect the caste identity. We desisted from this move, which would have ruined the reputation of the Indian Census, apart from creating an illegality under the Census Act by way of violation of the confidentiality clause!

India has a long tradition of modern Census-taking since 1871-72, which was a non-synchronous enumeration spread over a number of years preceding 1872. From 1881, Census become a synchronous one-time operation and has been held once every decade without break. The 1931 Census was the last one with detailed caste group enumeration. The 1941 Census in the midst of the Second World War was conducted with Gandhiji's call for cooperation on Census taking. The first linguistic survey of India spanning over the period 1898-1928 was the labour of love of an eminent Census officer (Dr. Grierson), who refused to go back to England until the survey was completed and reports were published. The scholarly Census reports and related studies (such as Hutton's) by the Census Commissioners of British India are legion.

A big leap in modern Census taking and converting the Census Organisation into a continuous permanent body with core staff was initiated by the 1961 Census Commissioner, Ashok Mitra. Mr. Mitra expanded the scope and content of Census and the post-Census surveys and studies such as longitudinal village and town studies, study of tribals, arts and crafts, temples, fairs and festivals and languages. He remained formally associated with these operations for over a decade. Though the Census-taking was further refined and improved, and the special studies continued in the next two Censuses, under the leadership of Chandrashekhar (1971 Commissioner) and Padmanabha (1981 Commissioner), none of these brilliant officers was allowed by the Government to continue in the Census Organisation beyond their five-years tenure or to be associated with the work in the way the 1961 Commissioner was permitted for a decade. Same way, I was not allowed to remain or be associated with the organisation formally beyond the tenure of five-years (1989- 1994). By and large, the inter-Censal Commissioners posted in the 1970s, 1980s or 1990s were not carrying the interest of the post- Census scholarly works or other technical aspects of the preparatory work for the next Census with zeal and vigour. This policy of Government for restricted tenure posting from the 1970s onwards has been counterproductive for smooth Census work and needs to be reviewed.

The 1981 Census initiated the use of technology for Census data processing through main-frame computer, and the 1991 Census took further steps by decentralised data entry in state and regional offices. The next two Censuses (2001 and 2011) have made further leaps into the use of advanced technologies, such as OMR quite well.

Indian Census over the last few decades has settled down well to the mixed de jure and de facto (or extended de facto) method of enumeration. The "Canvasser" method of questionnaire filling has remained the mode, as against the self-enumeration mode employed in some countries (such as the US). Even the USA is facing the limitation of non-response with the latter method, and had to follow-up through telephonic or door-to-door canvassing in cases of widespread non-response.

Canvassing tribe, caste (for Scheduled Caste) and religion is becoming more and more complex and political at times in some areas. So also is the case with mother-tongue and language. Census taking in crisis or conflict situations (Assam in 1981, J&K in 1991, Nagaland, Manipur and Naxalite areas from 2001 Census onwards) has proved to be a big challenge. The demand for data collection on controversial issues of caste/OBC, or specific constituencies of disability (2011), ex-servicemen (1991) has been becoming louder and louder. Sample Census Survey rather than full Census may be resorted in some cases.

Including some controversial issues such as 'caste' in enumeration is bound to turn the entire Census controversial and affect the quality of Census adversely. That was why the Home Minister of the 1951 Census, Sardar Vallabhbhai Patel and the Government of India made a principled decision not to do caste enumeration, except for scheduled castes. The pressure from some political circles in successive Censuses for OBC/caste enumeration was warded off until 2001 Census. In some tenuous way, the 2011 Census had to be associated with OBC/caste enumeration (survey) after the main Census. This does not augur well for the nation and the future of the Indian Census!

The politics of changing loyalties or alignments and manipulation for over or under count is confronted in case of eliciting data on religion, language or tribe/caste. The Census Organisation facing the challenge has to remain extremely vigilant, impartial and apolitical. Maintaining the accuracy, genuineness, neutrality and high quality of the basic demographic, economic and social data is extremely crucial. It is in this context that I am pleading for not overloading the Census with unnecessary and controversial data collection burden. Indian Census's good name should not be sullied or tarnished and its credibility in the eyes of the common people should not be compromised.

Based on my long association with the Census (since 1970), I would suggest the Census Commissioner to be made part of a Census Commission through a Constitutional Amendment with the required autonomy, professionalism and weightage, on the lines of the Election Commission. The model of the US Bureau of Census may also be studied in this connection.

The Final Round in the State Government (December 1994-March, 1997)

Chairman, IPICOL: A Short Stint

Towards the end of 1994, I was getting empanelled in my batch for promotion as Additional Secretary in the Government of India and was given two months' leave in Delhi to await my promotion. The process got unduly delayed and I was asked to revert to State Government by the end of November, 1994. I shifted to Bhubaneshwar and waited there for a fortnight before I was posted as a full time Chairman of the State Industrial Promotion and Investment Corporation. A decade earlier, I had served the same organisation as MD for four months. Being on familiar ground, I settled very quickly in the job and had a relaxed time as the MD, Mohan Kumar (now Secretary in Defence Ministry) was more into the nitty gritty of day to day operation. I had to take a rental accommodation in Nayapalli area as Government accommodation was denied.

This was for the first time that I worked under Chief Minister Biju Patnaik. When I paid a courtesy call on him, he recalled my earlier meeting with him in Delhi as Census Commissioner when he read from my Census report that

India was producing one Australia (in terms of population size) every year! He told me that this scenario of the size and growth of population prompted him to impose a two-child policy of disqualification in local bodies' election in the state. My pleading with him against such 'two-child norm' as anti-poor and anti-women and as counter-productive did not cut much ice. When I thanked him for posting me in IPICOL, he got confused and averred that I am posted to IDCOL – another public sector undertaking. He appeared to be confusing things – I did not see in him Biju Patnaik, the dynamic leader of earlier years. Election had just been announced and he was not in a good mood.

Not much initiative on new investment in early 1995 was possible as the State Assembly election had been announced. The hey-days of the 1980s holding out promising industrial investment were not there and a number of units had become sick. I could see a cautious and halting approach from the attitude of my colleagues in the Corporation. The initiative had been wrested from IPICOL by some senior Government and political bigwigs. One of the prominent Ministers close to the CM asked me to call the Chief Executives of all running industries to meet him! I did not appreciate this embarrassing move before the Assembly election and promptly refused to comply.

Principal Secretary to the State Government, Energy Department: Power Sector Reforms

In the election, Biju Patnaik's party was defeated and Congress came to power. J.B. Patnaik became the Chief Minister again – for the third time after a break of five years. In April, 1995, I was posted as the Principal Secretary in the Energy Department (and I continued, in addition, as IPICOL Chairman for a while).

My stint in the Energy Department for the next two years was very eventful, as I was associated with the big power sector reform and restructuring under way for a while. The newly elected Government was pro-reform in the same way as the earlier Government was. It was, therefore, not difficult to get political consensus. The restructuring plan got the nod from the Cabinet. The State Electricity Board was dismantled, and new corporate entities like Grid Corporation, Hydropower Corporation and Electricity distribution companies came up. There were many teething problems including adjustment of outstanding loans and the apprehension of staff and workers' unions.

We arranged many negotiation meetings, laid out the plan for quicker promotions and incentivised the structure of increments. Some went to courts of law. Luckily, we had taken pre-emptive moves and were not faced with any stay orders. The staff were mostly happy, and they benefitted.

The transition from Board to a Grid and Transmission Corporation in public sector was smooth, thanks to an excellent officer of 1963 IAS batch, M.Y. Rao being the Chairman of the Board and later the CMD of the Corporation. The intransigent stand of the Finance Department on the status of outstanding loans and liabilities and the World Bank's insistence for a time bound disinvestment and privatisation were not very wise decisions. As the later events in the Grid Corporation, Power Generation Corporation and Hydropower Corporation unfolded, our apprehensions became true.

In the earlier five year period, a large number of private power producers (many of them from abroad) had been invited to start projects (mostly thermal), and power purchase agreements had been negotiated. The demand of the State and regional grid was projected as very high based on prospective industries. Moreover, the overall approach to power purchase was mostly incentives for the producer's profit maximization, and not based on the capacity of consumers to pay. We had to re-negotiate the purchase agreements de-novo, even when some of these had already reached finality (like AES). From an average agreed level of Rs. 2.50 or more per unit, we succeeded to make them agree to less than Rs. 2 per unit. Our aim was to bring it down nearer to Rs. 1.55 or so. The Chief Minister, who was very happy with the re-negotiation, became restless, as we were bringing the rate down to below Rs. 2/-. There was a belief in the new Government that the earlier Government had compelled the negotiators to strike the deal at a higher purchase price on some political consideration. The new Government started realising that bringing down the purchase price to Rs. 1.55 or so will be a disincentive to the power producers. There was a feeling of relief among all concerned when I decided to go to the Government of India on promotion as Secretary after two years in April, 1997.

The story of privatised distribution companies was more complex. We wanted to go for a step-by step approach – a joint venture of sort followed by privatisation. The World Bank was opposed to this. We gave one region on a trial basis to BSES and it started working well. They, however, faced problems from the Government.

The OPGC's running thermal units, which were doing quite well, were handed over later to the US Company (AES) that also took a distribution area. I was opposed to this arrangement. The advice of expert Directors on OPGC Board, like Sachidanand Mishra and Bijaya Chandra Jena was very timely.

One of the key reform initiatives was the setting up of an independent Electricity Regulatory Commission. The bigwigs in the Government did not want to give up Government discretion. We worked through this mind-set and succeeded in setting up this institution. Some outstanding and honest officers like Somnath Som, Dhiren Ray and Bijay Jena were taken as members, and it appeared to be working well.

The Odisha model of power sector reform became a pioneering initiative and a talking point nationally and internationally. I was invited to Japan and many national fora to present this model and its operationalization. I have enclosed a write-up on Odisha Power Sector written recently (April, 2015) as Annexure-I.

As I was in the thick of it, my promotional empanelment as Secretary in the Government of India became known in early 1997. I was not being given a posting for three months on the plea that I am not likely to be spared by the State Government. This was explained to me by the Cabinet Secretary, TSR Subramaniam when I met him. He told me that one of Odisha Cadre batch mates, S. B. Mishra, who was posted as Secretary, Tourism, in the Government of India declined to join and the same might happen in my case. I assured him that it will not happen in my case, and that the State Government will definitely spare me. The Cabinet Secretary, however, dilly dallied and went on posting empanelled officers junior to me in the list. When I met him again, he said that as the vacancy of substantive Secretary was not available, I should accept a post equivalent to Secretary for a short period of three or four months, after which I would be given a substantive posting definitely. That's how I received an order of my posting as the Chief Commissioner, Investments and NRIs and Chairman, India Investment Centre in the Department of Economic Affairs, Ministry of Finance. Odisha Chief Minister, J.B. Patnaik, was initially unwilling to relieve me assuring that I would be promoted to Chief Secretary's rank soon, but I convinced him of my accepting the promotion at the Centre at that stage and he agreed. I was twice sounded and offered the post of Chief Secretary, Odisha – once in 1999 by Giridhar Gamango, the next Chief Minister and again when Naveen Patnaik (the present Chief Minister, Odisha) wanted a new Chief Secretary to replace my batch mate, S.M. Patnaik. I declined on both occasions, as I was comfortably settled in Delhi as a Secretary in the Government of India.

Before I left Odisha for Delhi, I went to Bishkek (Kyrgyzstan) on a brief UN advisory assignment in connection with Census taking in C.I.S. countries. Census and population subjects refused to leave me and remained my focal interest and specialization in a generalist management career in the IAS and even after my superannuation in the Government.

My mother, who was staying with me, expired in January, 1997, a few months before my departure for Delhi.

The Two Stalwart Patnaiks – Biju and J.B.

The style of administration differed remarkably between Biju and J.B. – both were visionary leaders with their own ideas and dreams; but they were diametrically opposite in their respective styles of administration and behaviour. Biju, with his initial entrepreneurial and adventurist days as an industrialist and daredevil pilot, came to Orissa politics with big vision of industrialisation and Paradeep port making, as a protégé of H.K. Mahtab, but outgrew the mentor and exhibited dynamism along with the least respect for administrative and financial propriety. He was a man in a hurry, impatient, impetuous and a bully at times with bureaucrats and advisors. He used to lose temper and spewed invectives, if targets were not met. For him, end justified the means. All this created an image of Biju as a leader with ferocity and unconventional methods, which brought some spectacular results for the state's development, but he was embroiled in controversy around favouritism, corruption and impropriety. He was much more subdued and temperate during his final tenure in State administration in the first half of the 1990s.

J.B. Patnaik, on the other hand, was quite balanced, level-headed, shy, urbane and reticent in his dealings in administration. He could be very Machiavellian in his intent and approach without exhibiting the ugly side. He did not show any emotion or sentiment, while taking tough measures against adversaries or enticing them to his advantage. While he was very close to a few Ministers and civil servants, he started working more independently in the second and third stints as Chief Minister. To keep his flock in the party owing allegiance to him together, he resorted to all means, thereby impinging on administrative propriety. Some of these strategies became his undoing and the people's disenchantment with his leadership and the Congress rule in the state. Biju babu's demise brought the sympathy wave for the Biju Janata Dal under Naveen Patnaik which has been thriving for more than three terms. Whether J.B. Patnaik's demise in April, 2015 will turn the tide of sympathy wave in the other direction, only the future will tell. There are many complex factors at work. It is difficult to predict the political future.

It is, however, certain to presume that there have been many positive stories of progress in Odisha over the last three or four decades, which can be attributed to many factors including stable governance under political leadership of some acumen. At the same time, many negative and short-sighted policies and strategies have been counter-productive to sustainable development and the well-being of the state and its people. Populist strategies might win people's vote in the short or medium term; but might be a canker to the soul of the state in the long run. Similar is the model of development based on indiscriminate exploitation of natural resources (such as mining or forest), which may show-case a few giant capital-intensive projects eliciting pleasure of some multinational companies and sudden spurt in GDP in statistical sense, but ultimately, it would cause long term disastrous consequences for the state and people (particularly tribals and the poor) in term of habitat, ecology and environmental decadence. Is it sustainable development? Should we go for limited employment and some infrastructure improvement and, in the process, invite large scale deforestation, desertification and dehumanisation contributing to adverse climate change? The top priority to be given to people's felt needs and sustainability appears to have been missing largely from the antenna of the leadership.

Harnessing State's resources in a rational and balanced manner would entail greater investment in small and marginal farming, meaningful linkages with village, small and medium industries, rational and imaginative exploitation of eco-tourism, skill building, emphasis on renewable energy, small and medium irrigation, conservation and rational exploitation of forest and mineral resources linked to tribal rights and ecology. The development model has to be the most forward-looking, when it comes to human resources – particularly education and primary health-care in a comprehensive manner – preventive, promotive, basic curative and rehabilitative for the poor, tribals, dalits and women.

Education linked to appropriate skill-building at every stage – primary, secondary and higher – must receive the top-most priority along with Primary Health.

Such alternative development model for states like Odisha with preponderance of poverty, tribals and dalits appears to be a better option than the over-ambitious paths of mega industrialisation, mega mining, mega power projects and mega higher-educational or tertiary health (medical) institutions. The mega-mania is a good start-up for show casing, but the adverse fall-outs are many, ending up with megalomania or delusions of grandeur, which is an insane passion for doing things on a very large scale. The concomitant generation of a few 'nouveau riche' (newly rich lacking social or intellectual standing) and black money spoiling the politics and society (the coal-chit fund-mining scams and crimes) at the expense of the interest of the common people and the environment is already staring at our face.

Final Round of Working in the Government of India (1997-2002)

Chairman, India Investment Centre and Ex-officio Secretary, Department of Economic Affairs

India Investment Centre, where I held my office as Chairman-cum-Chief Commissioner of Investment and NRIs between April, 1997 and July, 1999, was an institution of Government of India with a long and chequered history. It had its days of glorious highs with regional offices in the USA, UK, Europe,

Middle East and Singapore. These offices had been closed and the Indian missions abroad were catering to the work of the Centre. To attract Foreign Direct Investment and Institutional investment in general and NRI/PIO investment in particular, after the crisis of the early 1990s, the then Finance Minister, Manmohan Singh, took the initiative for creating the post of Chief Commissioner, Investment and NRIs at the level, rank and pay of a Secretary in the Department of Economic Affairs. With the status and experience of a Government of India Secretary and the corporate like flexibility and freedom of IIC as his instrument (IIC Board comprised the Finance Secretary, Industry Secretary, Commerce Secretary, External Affairs Secretary-Economic, Presidents, FICCI and CII presided over by him), this mechanism was meant to provide a co-ordinated investor friendly face to the potential foreign and NRI investors. Unfortunately, the web of vested interest in the bureaucracy and Ministries never liked this innovative instrumentality to be operationalized and take deep roots. It took quite a few years before a senior officer was posted in this position. Ajit Kumar of 1964 IAS batch found the going tough with insincerity and non-cooperation all-around, particularly from the Economic Affairs Department. He tried his best to make it work, but got disillusioned soon and was posted to Cabinet Secretariat and later as the Defence Secretary. I succeeded him as the second incumbent (there were, of course, illustrious predecessors in the rank of Additional Secretary heading as ED of IIC earlier, e.g., T. N. Chatruvedi and C.B. Jain). Little did I know when I joined that the Finance Minister (then Chidambaram) and Finance Secretary (then Montek Singh Ahluwalia) had already made up their mind to abolish the Centre and a cabinet note was awaiting approval.

When I convened the IIC Board meeting, I found that the Finance Secretary deputed his Joint Secretary, who was very negative and blocked all major decisions. The Industry and Commerce Secretaries sent their deputy secretaries. Only the Secretary (Economic) in External Affairs Ministry (Mr. Ram) was present and gave positive viewpoints. The representatives of FICCI and CII were pro-active.

And then came the Cabinet decision to close down the Centre, and I was directed to implement the decision relating to staff retrenchment without any benefit or adjustment in the Government after which I was to report to the Industry Secretary as the Chief Commissioner, Investments and NRIs. When I saw the cabinet note, I found that my predecessor had not been consulted nor was I, and it contained gross misrepresentation of facts about the functioning of the Centre and the Chief Commissioner. I met the Finance Secretary, Montek Singh Ahluwalia and the Finance Minister, Chidambaram, who did not like my comments and stuck to their stand. The IIC staff were very agitated and were planning to go to the court of law. It was at this juncture that my friend and great Shirdi Sai devotee, C.B. Satpathy predicted that the Centre would not be closed till I held the chair, and instead, the people who have done it would face ouster soon. This prediction came true. The Government fell and the next Government led by A.B. Vajpayee, with Yaswant Sinha as Finance Minister (and Vijay Kelkar as the new Finance Secretary), realised the worth of IIC, and took a fresh cabinet decision reversing the earlier decision, and ordered for strengthening the centre.

I organised the first Conference of prominent NRIs and PIOs in collaboration with FICCI. We made meticulous preparation inviting prominent NRIs and PIOs and potential foreign investors, going and meeting their groups or associations in person – from San Francisco, Los Angeles, New York, Chicago, Houston, Detroit, Toronto in the USA and Canada to London, Birmingham in the UK, Frankfurt in Germany, Hong Kong, Bangkok, Kuala Lumpur and Singapore, and Middle-eastern cities in a whirl-wind visit and investment road shows with the help of our foreign missions in a period of three months. I met bigwigs like Lakshmi Mittal, Swaraj Paul, Hindujas and many others, and extended our invitation to them to come to the conference in Delhi. Most of them attended the conference.

The Prime Minister Vajpayee, inaugurated the Conference and mingled and interacted with the NRIs/PIOs in an evening reception. This brought an upsurge of genuine interest from investors and we started taking follow-up. The PM announced the PIO Card, the possibility of dual citizenship and a slew of new policy declarations, which were investor friendly. I was visiting State capitals reviewing the pending FDI and NRI work with designated State Commissioners of Investments and NRIs. Meetings with the Central ministries and FIPB for follow-up were also organized. My friend of Mussoorie days, Vikram V Desai (on voluntary retirement from Indian Postal Service), helped me a great deal as Advisor, IIC.

We also became an active member of the international body on investment promotion (WIPO), which held a seminar in Geneva. Some of the State Investment Commissioners attended this seminar along with me. The DEA Secretary until recently, Arvind Mayaram, who was then the Rajasthan Investment Commissioner, had taken a very proactive role in galvanising the association in India.

As I had got too involved with the work in the IIC, I had forgotten the Cabinet Secretary's assurance of posting me as a substantive Secretary in three or four months' time. Almost two years had elapsed by then. The earlier Cabinet Secretary had once patted me saying that I was doing very good work in the IIC. So also the next Cabinet Secretary, Prabhat Kumar, who could not find a slot for me. Only the Principal Secretary to the PM (Brajesh Mishra) told me one day that the PM was very happy with the NRI conference and that I would be posted in a Ministry soon. In July, 1999, I was posted as Secretary, Department of Family Welfare in the Ministry of Health and Family Welfare.

My successors in the IIC did not stay for long and with the change of Government in 2004, the Finance Minister, Chidambaram put the axe on the IIC again. The NRI/PIO affairs went to a new Department of Overseas Affairs under the External Affairs Ministry to start with and later became a separate Ministry.

Thus ended my tryst with the destiny of India Investment Centre. Apart from attending to official work, I could, in places of my visit in India and abroad, come in contact with Shirdi Sai devotees and Sai centres. Some of my visits coincided with the opening of Shirdi Sai temples or important celebrations, where I had the pleasure of spending some time with C.B. Satpathy.

As Secretary, Ministry of Health and Family Welfare (1999-2002)

My final job in the Government sustained for close to three years till my superannuation in end-May 2002. This was a very fruitful and rewarding period. The Cabinet Secretary did not appear to be happy with my posting, and said that he had no say in my posting as it came from the Prime Minister. When Brajesh Mishra from the PMO had asked me for my preferences, I had given two preferences, namely, Department of Family Welfare and Department of Statistics on the ground of my specialisation, abiding interest and familiarity with population studies and census and surveys. I did not look for or be in the 'rat race' for high profile glamorous departments, like Mines, Power, Industry or Economic Affairs, even though I had worked in these sectors. The Cabinet Secretary thought that I had not worked formally in Health or Family Welfare and might not be suitable for it. He did not appreciate the organic link between this sector with my experience in Census and specialisation in population studies, policy and programmes. I wanted to contribute meaningfully to the population and development sector (Family Welfare as the nodal department) at the pinnacle of my bureaucratic career, apart from pursuing my academic-intellectual interest in population study. I had been sent feelers from a political leader (M.P.) (who was a Shirdi Sai devotee) about my posting in the Department of Revenue, if I accompanied him to the head of a prominent industrial house. I had declined to be part of this wheeler dealer move, which had become the order of the day!

In my 1991 Census reports, I had presented a balanced picture of the demographic transition under way in India and the States. While the decline in fertility had set in inexorably, projected to reach the replacement level by 2015-2020, the most worrying scenario was revealed as the declining sex ratio at birth becoming more and more skewed and adverse to females. My discussion with Amartya Sen in the early 90's (he used to come to my Census office for getting a feel of the fresh data for his forthcoming publications, where he gracefully recorded his acknowledgement of my ideas and thinking) spurred him to reinforce his 'missing women' and 'authoritarianism versus cooperation' hypotheses in population and development. The interstices of rights, entitlements, gender, capability and justice became clear to me, as I discussed with Amartya Sen, who wrote to me a letter complimenting me sky-high. That was, of course, before he won the Nobel Prize!

My background in Census, population surveys and demography helped me a great deal in my work in the Ministry of Health and Family Welfare. Many drafts of a national population policy were presented before me. I chose to redraft the policy, keeping in view the population scenario, the demographic transition under way, the issues of adverse sex ratio at birth, high infant, child and maternal mortality and reproductive morbidity, and the need for an inter-sectoral strategy and holistic goal of population and development came out loud and clear. The Group of Ministers were not quite happy with the holistic and 'soft' nature of this policy draft – they wanted more teeth and punch to 'control' population. The Cabinet meetings remained intense and inconclusive with sharp differences of opinion among the 'hawks' or hardliners, who wanted hard-hitting, authoritarian and quick-fix solutions, and the 'doves' and liberals, who agreed with me. I was given the job of convincing the 'hawks', which I did and hopefully it worked.

The National Population Policy, 2000 was approved by the Union Cabinet in February, 2000, and was placed in the Parliament. It received wide acceptance and recognition in national and international circles. India's population policy came in tune with the ICPD Programme of Action, by and large.

As a National Commission on Population was to be constituted, the Prime Minister's secretariat took it away from the nodal Health Ministry to the Planning Commission with a Member Secretary post created to adjust a relative of a senior officer of the Prime Minister's office. My reservation on such an arrangement to weaken the nodal Ministry implementing the population policy was not heeded. A parallel mechanism for implementation monitoring created ambivalence, confusion and chaos. Parliament questions were being handled by two organizations and contradictory replies were being prepared. With the intervention of the PM, it was decided that the Health Minister would reply to all Parliament questions on population and not the Planning Minister. The matter was finally resolved (after my departure), and the Commission has come back to where it was intended to be as per the policy – the Ministry of Health.

The Prime Minister's office constituted a 100 member Commission, which made it difficult to meet and be an effective body. The Commission was reconstituted after 2004, and the membership has been reduced to thirty odd. But it has met only twice. I continue to be a member of the Population Commission.

The 2001 Census confirmed my predictive analysis after 1991 Census on the population growth rate as well as the sex ratio at birth. So also the latest 2011 Census. The strategy and approach of the 2000 population policy became more relevant as the data of Census and the health and demographic surveys (SRS, NFHS and DHS/AHS) reflected. We got down to the task of making the State Governments agree to fine-tune their policies, strategies and programmes with the national policy.

Most of the State Governments consented. A few states, however, had included potentially coercive and counter-productive policies and strategies, like the two-child norm (Rajasthan, Orissa, Haryana, Madhya Pradesh, Himachal Pradesh and Andhra Pradesh). Letters were sent by the Union Health Minister to the Chief Ministers. The National Human Rights Commission also took it up. The matter bore fruit later, when I was part of a civil society advocacy group in my post-retirement assignment in Population Foundation of India and three State Governments (Haryana, Madhya Pradesh and HP) withdrew the two-child norm as a qualification for candidates for election in local bodies.

Along with UNFPA, we prepared advocacy material on population issues, and hosted advocacy seminars with elected legislators and other stakeholders. Dr. Francois Farah, Mr. Diego Garcia and Ms. Ena Singh from UNFPA as well as Dr. Almas Ali, an Advisor with UNFPA were very helpful in these efforts. While at the PFI after my retirement from the Government, we took intensive advocacy efforts with national judicial academy, media and legislators on the issue of female foeticide and rights based population programme with quality of care.

I was a votary for grassroots community-based plans for RCH-FP instead of top down target driven plans, which were unrealistic and potentially coercive. By the time I left the Government, we were getting community needs assessment done in at least 114 districts and more districts were about to fall in line. The proforma for monitoring review was modified to allow "Quality of Care" indicators to be incorporated, instead of targets of contraceptives (or Expected Level of Achievement) per se; but the old mind-set was very tough to change. It used to come back with a bang as soon as the efforts were relaxed!

We tried to put a brake on the 'camp' approach to family planning campaign (particularly, female sterilization). The dangers of the camp approach are well-known. Most of the

State Governments fell in line. We also gave a push to a basket of contraceptives, particularly no-scalpel vasectomy, IUD and condoms, with more training and better logistics of supply. Social marketing was encouraged. 'Informed Choice' was to be made real. Much to the chagrin of the leaders of Andhra Pradesh Government, we made it known to them that the camp approach to female sterilization at the very young age of 21 or 22 was not a healthy or safe option. But they were rejoicing at the sharp fall in fertility, which they, mistakenly attributed to their strategy of family planning by hook or crook! As studies of fertility transition in A.P. have shown, there was a combination of factors, and this strategy of controlling fertility was risky for women in the long run.

The issue of introducing injectables in the free public contraceptive distribution remained unresolved in my time, and continues so even now. I was told that many poor Muslim women look for injectables as the best option for them, as it is for women in Bangladesh, Indonesia and Iran. The way Net-en and implants were earlier handled by the Government, had cast a shadow over the introduction of DMPA injectables. Some women's groups were up in arms. ICMR's clinical trial reports had been kept under wraps, arousing suspicions all over. Even I was not shown these reports. We asked for further ICMR led trials in my time. The WHO's reports in other countries were O.K. Indonesia, Iran and Bangladesh went for stage by stage introduction. The only time I was trying to negotiate with the women's groups for stage by stage introduction, they grew suspicious. We succeeded in the withdrawal of stay order on Net-en from the Court, but could not succeed in introducing it. Of course, injectables are available in the private sector.

The issue of high infant and child mortality (in fact, a plateau in the rate for a few years in the 1990s had been noticed) was very mind boggling. The earlier efforts at childhood immunization had paid some dividends. But the neo-natal deaths had not come down much. The insistence of WHO for complete eradication of polio in a time bound manner through 'pulse' approach had been engaging the staff on this campaign to the detriment of all other programmes including the routine immunization. We had to strike a balance. However, polio was taking unduly large chunk of our time and resources. The WHO goal post of 2000 for polio eradication shifted to 2005. India was to become polio-free, but at what opportunity cost!

On our insistence, the World Bank agreed to support improvement of our routine immunisation programme, and a more realistic Reproductive and Child Health programme. The World Bank missions were quite frequent and were generally helpful in boosting our efforts. The RCH-I programme was very late in actual start-up in the States. The concept and philosophy of R.H. was very slow to sink in. The public health system, particularly at the primary health care level was in doldrums due to several factors including lack of adequate resources. The State Governments were not earmarking resources, and depended on the Central fund for family planning, immunisation and sub-centres. The concept of 'Health for All' or universal comprehensive primary health care had been practically given up, and verticalized disease-specific programmes were holding sway. Decentralized planning and monitoring were rarely attempted.

Even the Ministry of Health at the Centre and in major States were vertically divided into different silos right down to the field level. Such divisive and dichotomous outlook was not in the best interest of public health or primary health-care. Hence, our efforts were meeting with limited success on the ground.

Inter-agency coordination in the Pulse polio campaign posed a big challenge. I tried to hold weekly (Tuesday afternoon) meetings of heads of all national and international stakeholders. We were close to zero outbreak by 2001-2002; but things started becoming awry again, and eradication looked a distant goal. Chasing the goal became a passion, even among big civil society players like Rotary International.

Thanks to our renewed efforts at improving routine immunisation, and child health, IMR and under-five mortality started coming down from 2000. The initiative on maternal health under RCH helped in the reduction of MMR too. The statistics of 2000-2010 reflect the MMR situation, of late 90s and early 2000 decade.

I was very impressed with the community-based, women-empowered efforts at neonatal death reduction and cost effective new born care of Gadchiroli (Dr. Abhay Bang's experiment). This was published in the 'Lancet'. We invited Dr. Bang, visited the area and wanted to scale up the model across the country with appropriate training and mobilization. There was stiff resistance even from paediatricians' associations and some public health experts in WHO and UNICEF. I had to remain content with a multi-centric trial through ICMR, allotting funding from my department. Later on, in PFI, I tried to take advocacy with central and state governments for scaling it up under the NRHM and NIPI on the basis of promising results of trials. While NIPI sabotaged the initiative, the NRHM, under Prime Minister's and Planning Commission's directives, has taken it up with a stage by stage scaling up.

Another innovative initiative related to a new male contraceptive (RISUG)-safe and easy for adoption – had undergone important stages of ICMR trial for twenty years and was considered to be ready for marketing by 2002. A few days before my retirement, ICMR agreed to its introduction and announced the same in a meeting with the Health Minister, but went back on its words and created hurdles. The Delhi IIT scientist, Dr. Sujoy Guha – the inventor of RISUG, is waiting for a decade, going through further toxicity tests, although it was cleared from toxicity angle earlier. There is a sneaking suspicion of a conspiracy of sorts from the international lobby to delay its introduction.

I was quite lucky in reporting to the Health Ministers (there were four in succession), who had, by and large, been respectful to me and my views. In one instance of a Minister Shri Shanmugham, who was passing an order on some contraceptive purchase contrary to the settled procedure, I had to bring it to the notice of the Central Vigilance Commission and the PMO and the order was not carried out. The Minister was shifted to another portfolio. This Minister was candid enough to tell me that his job was at stake due to pressure from his party boss and my non-cooperation.

Apart from representing India in important meetings within the UN system, we were quite active in bilateral fora like DFID, USAID and European Commission, as well as third world fora like ICOMP (International Centre on Management of Population Programme), Kuala Lumpur (I was Vice-chair for a term) and PPD (Partners in Population and Development), Dacca. We developed excellent relations with reputed international non-government organisations, like the Population Council, McArthur Foundation, Ipas, Pacard Foundation, Rotary International, UN Foundation and Path, etc.

We had developed a transparent mechanism for regular interaction and collaboration with the civil society including the NGOs in India (the Mother NGO scheme), the women's groups, the academia, research bodies and the health and population activists. I had an open door policy and accepted invitations for attending important meetings organised by them.

The national institutions of importance – the International Institute of Population Science and the National Health and Family Welfare Institute – had their problems of identity, quality and autonomy. Being a part of their governing bodies, I took keen interest in their development. The Directors of these institutes (Dr. T.K. Roy and Dr. Kapilashrami, respectively) were given freedom and resources to run the institutes well. The involvement of IIPS in the second National Family Health Survey and District Household Surveys was very intense and a source of motivation and value addition for the faculty. An interesting programme of training of district level medical officers on public health management was introduced in NIHFW in collaboration with the European Commission, and the State Governments were brought on board to depute their medical officers.

Hindustan Latex Ltd was the only public sector corporation under the Department of Family Welfare. Its expansion and diversification was under way, along with quality and cost control. It started its foray into social marketing through a newly formed society known as HLFPPT. It started exporting some of its products. A proposal for its disinvestment was deferred. The Government had always a dilemma when it came to giving purchase preference to public sector's products. There was also attempt at political interference in the management of this company, which we did our best to ward off, with limited success.

The introduction of emergency contraceptive pills and medicated abortion pills was an initiative taken during my tenure with the development of appropriate protocols and instructions. We had series of meetings in this connection. Dr. Sunita Mittal, the Professor of OBGY in AIIMS, played a vital role in this initiative.

We started looking at the Medical Termination of Pregnancy Act and Rules for more effective implementation, and for amendments to simplify the registration process. We gave approval for a major study on safe abortion in India.

The issue of proper implementation of the Pre-natal Diagnostics Technique Regulation Act, 1994, came up in a big way in my time with a Public Interest Litigation filed by CEHAT, Mausum and Sabu George before Supreme Court. This PIL served in re-activising our monitoring of law enforcement in states and districts. The Supreme Court's directions made the Government wake up and look at the issue of pre-birth sex determination with sincerity. My consultation with activist Sabu George helped me to take a tough stand against the negligent States and districts. From my office in Nirman Bhavan, we guided crash teams to oversee and make surprise raids. A decoy operation in Faridabad district by the team led by Dr. Dahiya – the district authority (under my guidance and moral pressure) succeeded in unearthing two major cases of crime under the PNDT Act. The doctor's lobby made all efforts to wriggle out and put Dr. Dahiya in police station lock-up. Due to my timely intervention (telephoning Haryana CM's Secretary, Quereshi, who later became the Chief Election Commissioner) and persuading the Union Health Minister to write a congratulatory letter to the CM lauding his efforts in Faridabad), the concerned persons were arrested and cases were initiated. Dr. Dahiya was commended and later promoted as DG, Family Welfare, Haryana. Despite many hurdles in the prosecution and handling of these cases, we were successful in getting them convicted for sex determination. These were the first two cases of substantive conviction under the law in India, and some more have followed. The District authorities were trained, the Central and State Boards were galvanised and NGOs were involved for the two-pronged strategy of strict law enforcement and social re-engineering.

Towards the end of my tenure, as I was getting ready for retirement, I was pleasantly surprised that the FOGSI (Federation of OBGY associations) in their annual conference in 2002 conferred on me the Honorary Fellowship of the Indian College of Obstetrics and Gynaecology (ICOG) in recognition of my work on women's health! I was told that I was the first non-medical person in India to have been given this award. I continued to work on women's health and reproductive rights after my retirement from the Government.

My rapport with colleagues in the Ministry was quite healthy and amiable. We had very little problem of coordination among the three Departments of Health (headed by my batch mate Javid Chaudhary), Indigenous System (headed by 1966 batch officer Sailaja Chandra) and Family Welfare (headed by me), Directorate General of Health Services (headed by Dr. Agarwal), ICMR (Dr. Ganguly) and National AIDS Control Organization (headed by 1967 batch officer Prasada Rao). Same was the case within my Department – the two Joint Secretaries, (Gautam Basu and Meenakshi Dutta Ghosh) Deputy

Commissioners, Directors, Deputy Secretaries, Assistant Commissioners and other staff. They extended cooperation, support and guidance to me in a spirit of team work, and I recognised the role and contribution of each member of the staff and their teams.

I was equally fortunate in getting excellent support and cooperation from many stalwarts from the civil society, academic-research community, media and the UN and bilateral institutions. Even MPs like Shabana Azmi and Rajiv Rudy, who were interested in a holistic population policy, lobbied with other MPs and the Prime Minister. Gita Sen from IIM, Bangalore, Leela Visaria, Saroj Pachauri (Pop Council), Poonam Muttereja (MacArthur Foundation), Anjali Nayyar, Vimala Ramachandran led 'Health Watch', Veena Majumdar, Avabai Wadia and Nalini Abraham (Plan) and many other stalwarts were supportive of our strategy, and mentored me in many ways towards gender-sensitivity. Prema Ramachandran was very helpful from the Planning Commission. Prominent organisations like Plan, Family Planning Association, Voluntary Health Association of India, Population Foundation of India, CINI, Gandhigram Institute, Dr. N.H. Antia, Dr. Raj Arole, CHETNA and SEWA were the most helpful. Professor Ranjit Roy Choudhury, Dr. Sujaya Guha and Dr. M.K. Bhan were my mentors in the research work of the Ministry.

Camaraderie in the Working Career of IAS

I was very close to many civil servants of 1964 and 1965 batches of direct IAS, having been part of the training in the Mussoorie Academy in 1964 as well as 1965-66. I have been attending some of the batch mate get-togethers of both these batches since 1989 and I feel more at home with the 1964 batch colleagues. Having worked in the Odisha cadre, I developed more frequent interactions with Sahdev, Lakshmidhar, Bhaskar, Satyaranjan, Pritiman (he is no more), Sanujit, Durga Prasad (he is no more) and Pratap (he is no more). Similarly, the 1965 batch cadre mates like Sudhanshu Mishra, Sudhanshu Patnaik, Somnath, Rabi, Kalyan, Kailash (he is no more), Santosh Rao (he is no more) and Abhaya Rath are close to me. Among the senior colleagues of Odisha cadre with whom I have enjoyed interacting are R. K. Bhujabal, Pyari Mahapatra, Surendra Mishra, M.Y. Rao, Ashok Mubayi (he is no more), Radhakant Nayak, Nilamadhab Mahanty, P. C. Hota, F.A. Moses (he is no more), S.K. Basu (he is no more), M.P. Modi (he is no more), Sitakant Mahapatra, Somanath Som, Ram Upadesh Singh (Bihar cadre), S.K. Lal. Nihar Hota, Sovan Kanungo, D.K. Chatterjee, R.N. Das, Premananda Tripathy, J.K. Bhattacharya, J.P. Das, R.K. Rath, R.K. Mishra, Sushanta Palit (he is no more), K. Srinivasan (he is no more), Bhupender Singh, Sunderrajan, L.I. Parija, Venkataraman, U.C. Aggarwal, B. R. Patel (he is no more), B.C. Mathur (he is no more) and R. Srinivasan (he is no more). Among the younger colleagues of Odisha cadre, I recall my interaction with D.P. Bagchi (my classmate and friend from college days), Vivek Patnaik, Vinod Jha (he is no more), Samar Mahapatra, Sunil Patnaik (now a Sanyasi), Prasanna Mishra, Sarita, Sanjiv Hota, Purkait, Srinivas Rath, Pratip Mahanty, Dinesh Gupta, Santosh Nautiyal, Madan Mahanty, Ashok Mishra, D.N. Padhi, Harmohan (he is no more), Ajit Tripathy, Chahar, Subash Pani, Rabi Senapati, Himanshu, Satish Agnihotri and many more. Also, Ashok Mahapatra (Himachal cadre), Suresh Panda (Assam cadre), Khitish Mahapatra (Gujarat cadre), Ramesh Ray (Railways) Amar Mishra, Dhiren Ray and Swarup Parija the last three from the IRS.

Satsang Connections

The SAI family is a strongly bonded relationship of 'rinanubandh' based on common emotive devotion bereft of material considerations of 'give and take'. The ethos and values are solely spiritual. From the village folks of Tigiria like Tuna or Gopali to the likes of Purna Panda, Pari Mishra, Kishore Satpathy, or Satya Khadagray of Bhubaneshwar,

Cuttack area to the many devotion soaked hearts of Delhi – Noida-Moradabad-Mumbai-Tirupati-Nagpur (like Chhabras, Kumkum Bhatia, Sangita, Hari Kapur, Manoj Sinha, Aasha Kapur Mehta, and many others) to all over India and world (From Assam to Jammu, from Dehradun to Kanya Kumari) and from the USA to Malaysia, Indonesia, Singapore, from Europe to Australia, New Zealand and Africa, I have experienced the effervescence of eternal SAI phenomenon and consciousness binding all of us with ethos and bliss, which we share and value as our unique treasure in life. No other association or relationship in life's gross journey can be compared to this bonding of devotional emotion sans mundane considerations.

There are a few souls, who have evolved spiritually, with whom I am connected by the grace of Sadguru. Apart from the ardent Sai devotee, Shri C.B. Satpathy, with whom I am fortunate to be connected since 1975 (more spiritually since 1989), I get connected with Swami Nirliptananda of Divine Life Society, Rishikesh; Swami Nijananda Saraswati of Odisha, Shri Madhusudan Pati (a disciple of Swami Chidananda Saraswati), who has written two excellent books on the Upanishads, Bhagavata Purana and Guru Archana and Shri Premananda Tripathy (writer of a book on Yoga Sadhana). By God's design and Sadguru's grace, soul mates are connected.

8

Activism Within Civil Society (2002-2015)

As ED, Population Foundation of India (2002-2010)

An opportunity to work on rights-based and gender-sensitive population and health programmes within the civil society nationally and internationally came my way, when I was offered the position of Executive Director of Population Foundation of India – a non-government foundation established way back in 1970 by a group of philanthropists and social thinkers led by J.R.D. Tata, the scion of the Tata industrial house. I joined the Foundation in August, 2002 after getting the required clearance from the Government relating to post-retirement assignment. I was the fifth E.D. (after Kavoori, Padmanabha, Harish Khanna and Srinivasan) of the Foundation, which was supporting civil society initiatives on population programmes and advocacy on population issues.

I was in two minds when it came to accept any job at this juncture. There was the calling from my Spiritual Master –

Shirdi Sai Baba – to look inward after all these years of gross worldly action. I did not have the need for earning money, having completed my family responsibilities of settling my three daughters. I did not have any more craze for name or fame. I had, however, a sneaking desire to play the role of an activist in the civil society unencumbered by restrictions or control from the Government. May be this unfulfilled desire was being given a chance for fulfilment through this new assignment! That's how Sadguru makes you act and satisfy your legitimate desire! As my spiritual mentor, C.B. Satpathy told me then: "Behind every work that Sadguru gives you, there is a spiritual purport and dimension. One has to recognise this subtle game."

I settled down to the Foundation's work in a few months. My predecessors had laid the foundation for transition from stand-alone family planning to 'population' to a considerable extent. But I found that some Board and Advisory Council members, as well as staff were not yet sensitive to the paradigm shift in the concept of population and development. Their attitude to population issues was primarily one of the neo-Malthusian 'population control' modes. Reorienting their mind set was my biggest challenge. They would always ask me of every proposal as to 'Where is family planning? Some Board members, who understood the paradigm shift, were not able to convince the prominent members. The mantle fell on me to explain again and again that family planning integrated organically within Reproductive Health and Rights in Primary Health Care and equitable social development is the most effective strategy for tackling the population problem, and that the same is the main strategy of the National Population Policy, 2000. It did make sense to them for some time; but they would again revert to their old mind-set. Some ill-informed senior officers from the Government, including one Health Secretary, Prasanna Hota, added fuel to the fire by contaminating their mind against my interpretation of the population issue.

Despite this reservation, the Board gave full support to me in my efforts at making PFI more relevant and prominent as a vanguard of civil society advocacy on population issues. The Board members, who were appreciative of my ideas on the population issue and gave consistent support, were Avabai Wadia (she is no more) M.S. Swaminathan, Ranjit Roy Choudhury (he is no more), J.C. Pant, Leila Seth and B.G. Verghese (he is no more). The Board Chair, Vice-Chair and other members would appreciate off and on, but were not fully on board on looking at population issues from the prism of rights, gender and development. They were either grudgingly giving support or were neutral and indifferent. The Board Chair, Dr. Bharat Ram – a nonagenarian was initially unhappy with my ideas and style of functioning, but got very fond of me and came to the Board meeting in December, 2006 despite his sickness to persuade the Board to give me an extension of three years beyond July 2007. He died in July, 2007 before I was detected with cancer. The next Board Chair, Hari Shankar Singhania, got scared of my illness and wanted to look for a successor in my place, giving a hint to me to resign. I was, however, on my legs soon after surgery and was able to carry on the Foundation's work actively, which helped me to recover quickly. Mr. Singhania and other Board members were happy with my quick turnaround and recovery.

As I look back, I feel satisfied for making PFI better known nationally and internationally. The turnover of funding went up manifold from the level of Rs. five crore annually in 2002 to around Rs. 80 crore when I left in 2010. PFI, apart from being a very prominent civil society player on family planning and population issues, became the most eligible to lead a consortium with funding support for HIV/AIDS projects and urban health for the poor. We could, through very hard work of project formulation, compete successfully for garnering substantial resources from the Global Fund, USAID and some international and national donor agencies.

The quality of work within the PFI and its partners and grantee civil society players improved considerably. The PFI staff got oriented in modern techniques of project formulation, appraisal, monitoring and evidence based advocacy and communication. From a staff strength of about thirty in 2002, it went up to over one hundred with regional and state offices being opened at many places. The PFI core staff were given a chance to work hands on in the field with collaborating partner organisations jointly.

Advocacy work became more sharp and noticeable. Apart from policy advocacy through regular regional and state level workshops, there were issue-based advocacy seminars. Networks of advocacy orgaizations on issues were formed and communication strategies were attuned appropriately. The backroom activities of PFI in the formulation of NRHM, and a strong community action group were recognised both within and outside the Government. PFI's initiative in Bihar, Jharkhand, Odisha and Chhattisgarh were well-recognised.

Though majority of the Advisory Council's members led by M.S. Swaminathan were supportive of our strategy and gave constructive suggestions, there were some (including a retired bureaucrat, T.V. Antony), who were very hostile to our strategy, to say the least. These obstructionists, I am told, have not been re-elected to the Council after my departure. My successor, Poonam Muttreja is continuing the strategy with zeal.

During my tenure in the PFI, I was taken as a temporary advisor for two years in WHO's international committee on Reproductive Health Research. I attended one week of annual committee's meeting in Geneva and pleaded for the recognition of research on new contraceptives of safe and non-hormonal type, like RISUG in India.

I was in the international advisory committee of Lucile and Pacard Foundation, Palo Alto, California for a period of six years. I was also for six years on the Board of Ipas – a prominent NGO working on safe abortion and reproductive rights internationally headquartered in North Carolina, USA. Ipas has been working in India in a big way. All this kept me updated on international thinking on population issues, and to be a part of civil society activism on Family Planning, Reproductive Health and Rights.

One of the key staff in PFI, Ramaseshan, who was the Secretary and Treasurer, up to my retirement, had assisted me honestly and sincerely in my good and bad days in PFI. He was a tower of strength to me and to PFI. We used to share many ideas and visions for the organisation. He used to be very cautious in financial matters, and believed in the adage: "Every paisa saved is a paisa earned". He was an avid student of Bhagavad Gita. He has left us for his heavenly abode in December, 2012. Another soul mate during the PFI days, Dr. Almas Ali had an accidental death in October, 2012. He worked in PFI as a Senior Advisor until my departure. Both Ramaseshan and Almas Ali were great assets for PFI. It is a great personal loss for me. Incidentally, Dr. Ali co-authored with me 'Advocacy Papers' published by PFI in 2010, and the chapter on Health and Population for the first Social Development Report in India, a few years earlier.

Towards the end of my tenure in the PFI, I became the Board Chair of CHETNA, an NGO based in Ahmedabad and a founding Board member of 'World Health Partners'. After retiring from the PFI, I am on the Board of 'Centre for Health and Social Justice', 'Pathfinder India', and 'Freedom From Hunger, India' apart from being on the advisory committee of 'Global Health Strategy' and the Vice Chair of the Board of National Coalition on Food and Nutrition Security and Chairperson of the Coalition against Two-child Norm and Coercive Population Policies. These works are honorary and part-time. I do not intend to go back for any paid job or full time work. I do advise informally through an 'Advocacy Resources Network' and Grass Root Support Foundation formed by my activist academic daughter, Bijayalaxmi, with whose family I live now in Delhi.

Activism and Support for Some Social Causes: Building Institutions in Civil Society

As I experienced the realities of the issues around health, population and social development of the poor and the marginalised more and more, working earlier in the government and more intensively in the project areas of the Population Foundation of India, as well as policy advocacy efforts of the national and international rights and gender based networks, I was invited to lead or be a member in some prominent networks, coalitions or alliances. I also got invitations from some national and international non-government organisations to join their boards or councils. In some cases, I became a founding member/trustee/director of such institutions as they were formed. This had happened even when I functioned as the Execution Director of PFI (2002-2010), and more since 2011.

There exists a vibrant rights-based international network holding 'Asia-Pacific Conference on Reproductive Health' (APCRH) at regular intervals of three years. I was elected to be the Chairperson of the conference, when the India network was elected to host and organise the conference in 2007. More than one thousand delegates from at least 100 countries attended the conference. The organising committee wanted the PFI to be the conference secretariat, as there was some reservation about some other organisations, which had shown interest. As a gesture of compromise and goodwill, I prevailed on the members to accept Family Planning Association of India as the secretariat, even when I worked as the Chair and extended all support from the PFI. In the process, there was support and bonhomie from all other organisations throughout the planning and organising phases. We ensured fair play in the selection of papers for presentation through peer reviews and an impartial working group headed by Saroj Pachauri – the

Regional Director of Population Council. Mobilising resources was a tough job, but we were lucky to achieve our target thanks to the initiative of Madhubala Nath of IPPF. A venue at the biggest complex at Hyderabad was selected, as no such venue was available in Delhi or Mumbai then. Meticulous details of all arrangements were attended to, as we were inching towards the D-day in October, 2007. The conference went off very well, even though I could not attend the same, as I went through cancer surgery and the first chemotherapy cycle in September-October, 2007. I requested the Vice Chairs to manage in my absence. China was elected as the host organiser of the next APCRSH Conference, and I continued to play some role as a member of the next international organising committee.

The themes in this conference were focussed on adolescence and young people. India and some countries of Asia-Pacific have been faced with a youthful population with the possibility of reaping the 'Demographic Dividend' in the next two or three decades, before this transition passes towards demographic ageing in varying degrees; such a transition has been or is becoming a phenomenon in China, Japan and many western countries. The sexual and reproductive health needs get re-prioritized accordingly. The dynamic needs of the present and the emerging needs of the transition process have to be assessed and taken care of. The policies, strategies and the programmes of the governments in the respective regions have to be attuned to these demographic and health transition imperatives. The status quo in the mind-set with an obsession with neo-Malthusian strands on Population issue and with obstinate over-emphasis on terminal methods of family planning (mostly for women) bereft of Quality of Care is the most obsolete and irrelevant strategisation in countries such as India. This was one of the main refrains of the conference, apart from many other points relating to different countries and variegated aspects of Reproductive and Sexual health, including HIV/AIDS and sexual minorities.

Earlier, in 2004, I had, through an oration in the annual gathering of the demographers at Annamalai University in Tamil Nadu, and my convocation address at the International Institute of Population Science at Mumbai, presented a strong critique of the neo-Malthusian mind-set in the population programme implementation, which was not to the liking of the then Family Welfare Secretary (P.K. Hota). He thought that some of us speaking the new languages of reproductive rights and gender sensitive programme of Family Planning had been influenced by UNFPA, which was not in the best interest of the targeted Family Planning programme revived by him. He took the cudgel against the rights based policies, which were very much in tune with the National Population Policy, 2000 and was misguided by a long time retired bureaucrat (T.V. Antony) and some neo-Malthusian demographers to follow the old, obsolescent path of population control, discarded a decade back in the international and national policy frameworks. The senior functionaries in local UNFPA, who were not to his liking, had to leave India, and the new incumbents had to toe or tread his line very cautiously.

It was at this juncture in 2004 and 2005 that the designing of the National Rural Health Mission was being discussed in the Government and at the National Advisory Council presided over by Sonia Gandhi. Prior to the 2004 Parliamentary elections, the Vajpayee Government was coming under pressure from the hard core hawkish lobby to formally impose a two-child norm policy and bring back targeted contraceptive (sterilisation) programme with Sushma Swaraj as Union Health Minister and P.K. Hota as Family Welfare Secretary. They were not able to materialise their design due to strong civil society activism and Vajpayee's liberal ideas.

The Congress Manifesto for 2004 election contained many progressive and gender sensitive measures; but the one on targeted family planning smacked of regressive neo-Malthusian mind-set. After the UPA Government come to power, a civil society group took up the issue with Sonia Gandhi, who was convinced of the mistake in the manifesto and took measures to rectify with a clarification to all concerned.

While the NRHM design was being discussed in the National Advisory Council, some of us were invited to participate in the discussion. We ensured that the initial proposal to use NRHM as an instrument of targeted Family Planning was put at naught and, instead, maternal health with emphasis on improving institutional and safe delivery was introduced as the main thrust of the flagship programme of NRHM. The contribution of stalwarts like Dr. N.H. Antia with easy access to the Prime Minister and the pro-Left lobby of academia in JNU and Veena Mazumdar from the CWDS were very notable in the advocacy efforts of the civil society. PFI played a key role in providing support in this direction.

The NRHM documents as finally adopted by the Government of India were saved from a disaster of regressive obsolescence in the programmatic strategy. The re-emphasis on integrated health services with the primacy of Primary Health Care and increased investment on infrastructure in accordance with the objective of 'architectural corrections' was a very welcome step hailed by the civil society. In practice, however, selective disease-specific health care approach continued to plague the fledgling health system. The priority given to the reduction of maternal mortality and infant and child mortality was unassailable. But the sole resort to complete institutional delivery by hook or by crook to the exclusion or rejection of other community based 'safe' delivery mechanisms including re-arming of traditional birth attendants, nurses and midwives has met with partial success. The cost-effectiveness and sustainability of the approach with half-baked and ill-conceived allurement of financial incentives and in the absence of proper manpower and infrastructure is seriously in question.

The civil society activism of People's Health Movement (Jan Swasthya Abhiyan) and other fora had decided to constitute strong Community Vigilante Action Groups at community, district, state and national levels to closely monitor the NRHM work. Dr. N.H. Antia was in regular contact with me and a few other activists in this regard. The Mission Director of NRHM, Mrs. Jalaja and Joint Secretary, Amarjeet Sinha appreciated the move and requested Dr. Antia and me to help the Government recognise and support the communitization process through the constitution of a National Advisory Group on Community Action for NRHM, with a civil society secretariat at the PFI. A 21- member group was constituted and notified as Govt-Civil Society initiative soon after the NRHM was launched. The mechanisms at state, district and village levels were designed. The Village Health, Nutrition and Sanitation Committees with PRI and community-based support were formed gradually to be trained and empowered. A pilot in seven states was implemented by the AGCA with PFI as the secretariat for over two years and the modules and framework of community-based monitoring of health services were formulated, field-tested and evaluated. This was spear-headed by PFI and Centre for Health and Social Justice (CHSJ) (Dr. Abhijit Das), and the members of AGCA in various states. There have been initial misunderstandings, misgivings and resistance from the health service providers and managers; but these got ironed out, when they saw better results and satisfaction from the community.

The AGCA has been meeting regularly every quarter since its formation, along with full Government support and recognition. Its advice on the communitization process is taken seriously by the Government of India. The State Governments are by and large coming into terms with the process, though there is still a problem with allocation of resources. I have continued to be a member of the Advisory Group on Community Action even after I relinquished the charge of ED, PFI in September, 2010. This institution with many stalwarts of Public Health activism as members continues to work with vibrancy, and PFI continues to be the national secretariat for a decade or so.

My commitments for rights-based and gender-sensitive Population, Health and Social Development strategies drove me to update my knowledge of the subject and issues internationally. Apart from reading peer-reviewed journals such as 'Population and Development Review', 'Population Studies', 'Demography', 'Reproductive Health Matters' and 'Family Planning Perspective', I went through many books and documents. A History Professor from USA, Matthew Connelly has written a book on Population Control, which has been published in 2008 by Harvard University Press, titled *Fatal Misconception: Struggle to Control World Population*. Matthew spent some time in Delhi in 2005 or 2006, and discussed with me many issues in India's history of family planning; I helped him in clarifying many issues including sharing a copy of my oration in the annual IASP Conference in 2004, titled "Obsolescence and Anachronism of Population Control: From Demography to Demology". This oration has been published in *Demography India* – the journal of the Indian Association of Study on Population, and republished in *Population Advocacy Papers*, published by the PFI in 2010.

In the annual Ved Prakash Oration of the National Institute of Health and Family Welfare, New Delhi on 3 December 2014, I spoke on "Population Problem: Myths and Realities". A copy of this oration is presented in the annexure of this book to familiarise and share with the readers the spirit of a rights-based and gender-sensitive conceptualisation of the misunderstood issues of Population.

Since 2010, a "National Coalition against Two-child Norm and Coercive Population Policies" has been formed with initial support from the Hunger Project. I was invited to this forum to be the Chairperson. The Centre for Health and Social Justice – a national NGO with Dr. Abhijit Das as the Managing Trustee – is the national secretariat of this coalition. There are activist, NGOs and individuals in a few states, who are members of this coalition.

The Hunger Project supported this Coalition due to its concern with political disempowerment of the poor women in the Panchayati Raj institutions in states, such as Odisha and Rajasthan, where a statutory two-child norm disqualifies men and women, who have more than two children to stand or continue as elected members of any panchayat or urban local body. Policy advocacy with the concerned State Governments has been going on without success so far. Sustained advocacy and mobilisation of public opinion has been going on. Similar efforts during the last decade and half by the civil society have succeeded in State Governments of Himachal Pradesh, Haryana and Madhya Pradesh withdrawing the two-child norm as disqualification for election to PRIs/ urban local bodies. The coalition has also worked in Bihar and UP when similar two-child norm was being contemplated in the Panchayat elections. Apart from political participation, there are measures of two-child norm in many other vital schemes of welfare impinging the poor and disadvantaged communities very adversely. Restrictive norms like one or two child policy have been counterproductive, anti-poor, anti-women, apart from exacerbating adverse sex ratio at birth, as evidenced in China and India. Hence, the Coalition's advocacy and mobilisation strategy is in public interest and needs the support of all concerned citizens.

The other dimension of the Coalition's work relates to advocacy against violation of human rights, dignity, privacy and well-being of people by state agencies through pursuing coercive or potentially coercive population control policies, strategies or programmes. Some current practices pursued by the Government or service providers, such as 'targeted' contraceptive delivery, (particularly of female sterilization) in 'camps' without 'Quality of Care', informed choice and follow-up, resulting in long term morbidity or even death. Although contraceptive 'targets' have been abolished since 1996, and are banned under the National Population Policy, the 'targetisis psychosis' of authoritarianism comes to the fore in the newly coined euphemistic language of 'Expected Level of Achievement' computed on some strange demographic formula in the Statistics Division of Nirman Bhawan (Health Ministry's office in Delhi) communicated down to the states, districts and blocks. The alternative mechanism of preparation of bottom-up work plan based on the assessment of community needs in each village or ward of an urban area, as was envisaged in the National Population Policy, has not been tried with sincerity and rigour, except in a few districts. The assessment of work of health service managers and frontline workers being linked to such top-down targets (or ELA), and rewards or penalties (including financial incentives) being the order of the day, the easiest option is resorted to, namely, female sterilisation camps with record number of operations and surgery in two or three hours in the evening by a gynae surgeon, who does not have the time, inclination or resources to stick to the principle of informed choice or the Quality of Care guidelines. They (both the provider and the beneficiary), being torn between the devil and the deep sea, choose the former. Is it not 'coercive' family planning service?

The Civil Society Coalition chaired by me advocates against such coercive programme strategies, mobilises public opinion in favour of a sensible rights-based and gender sensitive population policy, monitors family planning programmes and exposes adverse events through trained activist volunteers. If required, Public Interest Litigations are filed in the Supreme Court.

Integrally linked with the issue of Population Stabilisation is the phenomenon of decline in sex ratio at birth, reflecting son preference, daughter aversion and misuse of technology for pre-birth sex determination, leading to sex selective abortions. In a national seminar in 2002, I had gone to the extent of expressing a viewpoint that it does not matter if population stabilisation is delayed by a decade or two; but it does matter if the adverse sex ratio at birth is arrested and reversed in the process. A sex-ratio balanced stabilisation of population by the latter half of the 21st century will avert a demographic and social disaster. The *Seminar* journal, January, 2002 carried my speech. This was when I was still working as the Secretary, Ministry of Health and Family Welfare!

As I have stated earlier, my PFI stint during 2002-2010 provided me ample opportunity to build advocacy and social mobilisation networks to address the issue of Sex-selective Abortion with all its legal and social ramifications. I am now happy to see the Prime Minister, Narendra Modi's clarion call for saving the girl child (*Beti Bachao*). I was invited by the Modi Government to address the Ministers and Secretaries concerned from the Centre and selected states on the issue at Panipat (Haryana), where the Prime Minister was launching the *Beti Bachao* Campaign on 21-22 January 2015.

I spoke of my tryst with the law on pre-birth sex determination (PCPNDT Act) since 1991 Census days, and presented some practical suggestions to make a success of law enforcement. I am enclosing a summary of my address and power-point presentation as an Annexure.

My eldest daughter, Bijayalaxmi, who teaches in Miranda House (Delhi University), has done extensive research on the issue of sex selective abortion in the wider context of gender and state, and has been continuing a campaign among teachers and students since 2002 under the caption of CAPF (Campaign Against Pre-birth Elimination of Females) in Delhi. Being a member of State Supervisory Board of Delhi Government under PC-PNDT Act for a few years, she has inside knowledge of the law enforcement situation. She has started an NGO 'GRSF' (Grass Root Support Foundation) on the issues of women of which the campaign against the Sex Selective Abortion is an important programme. I do advise GRSF, as and when asked for.

Another important civil society institution, which has been built over 2007-2015 in India under the leadership of Professor M.S. Swaminathan (the eminent agriculture scientist and father of Green Revolution) is the National Coalition on Food and Nutrition Security. Prof. Swaminathan, who was the Chairperson of the Advisory Council of Population Foundation of India, requested me in 2009 to be a convenor of a Task Force on Governance and Coordination in the Coalition on Nutrition Security. That's how I became a part of this vital institution building. The recommendations of the Task Force chaired by me were approved by the Coalition Steering Committee and the new organisation was formally registered in 2014. I was elected as the Board Vice Chair and a founding member.

The interim secretariat is with Save the Children, but the Coalition is transiting to its own independent setup in 2016. A strategy vision document has been prepared and many activities have been planned. Food and nutrition security linked with health, hygiene, sanitation and agriculture is being advocated within a rights-based framework. Many international, national and local organisations and individuals have joined the coalition. I am chairing a Screening and Ethics Committee charged with the responsibility of fixing norms of selection of membership keeping in view conflicts of interest and other ethical concerns. The coalition has been able to formulate Leadership Agenda of Action and Block Operational Plans of Action. It has worked so far with Government representatives from Health, Women and Child Development and Food Ministries as well as Planning Commission (now replaced by Niti Ayog), and National Institute of Nutrition, etc. Many researchers and academia are members in addition to UN institutions and NGOs. The coalition will not implement projects, but will be a knowledge hub of evidence for carrying on advocacy along with its members on various aspects of food and nutrition security.

Three other new civil society institutions where I became founding member/Director/Trustee are World Health Partners (WHP), Freedom from Hunger India Trust and Pathfinder International India. While the first and the last one work on reproductive health, family planning and health in general, the second organisation integrates livelihood, credit, income of community groups of the poor organised by Micro finance institutions/Self Help Groups/NGOs with health education, including nutrition, sanitation and MCH.

'World Health Partners' is the brain-child of Gopi Gopalakrishnan, a highly innovative social entrepreneur, who made a distinct dent in the very difficult state of Bihar (undivided) in the late 1990s through the innovative 'Janani' programme for better maternal health, family planning and safe abortion. He worked in Vietnam and came back to India to start the new organisation, which works intensively in a number of districts in UP and Bihar on innovative approaches to health and family planning services. Gopi invited me to join as a founding Board member. There are interesting programmes of primary health care with telemedicine referrals and use of IT and mobile phones. Partnership with state governments has been built up where reproductive health is a priority. Support from Warren Buffet and Bill and Melinda Gates Foundation has been quite helpful.

While I have mostly been a backstage player in all these Civil Society movements and institution-building because of my commitment to and passion for these contemporary social causes nationally and internationally, I have never tried to get too much involved mentally or to elicit any mileage in terms of honour, position or recognition. With a sense of non-attachment, I play my role as it comes. My intention is not to vault any ambition for glorification or martyrdom, but to give back to society what I feel right. The bright minds of the new generation would do a much better job. The little sensitivity and passion that, as part of the elderly crowd of social enterprise practitioners with exposure to the working of the Government and civil society, have been ingrained in us will hopefully be of some utility to the society.

9

Marriage and Family

The selection of my life partner (wife) in mid 1965 was made through a consensus arrived at by my parents, elder sister (Bidyutlata) and me. Manorama came from a joint extended family of 'Kar' clan from Tilabindha Jignipur village in Cuttack district, who were living under a common kitchen in Cuttack city and owned the Saraswat Press and the *Matrubhumi* daily newspaper. She was well-suited to adjust to my family with a number of brothers and sisters, with her mental disposition of straight forward dealings, frankness, magnanimity and simplicity. Her father, Narasimaha Kar, had risen from his 'Banar Sena' (Child soldiers of freedom movement) days through tutelage under idealistic leaders of the Communist movement, like Bhagwati Prasad Panigrahi to the building of public institutions like Salipur College, Primary Health Centre, and the daredevil, independent Odia daily, *Matrubhumi*, which he took to great heights. He was a stern disciplinarian with ethical principles, which he never compromised and dissociated himself from all these institutions after some time. His entrepreneurial skills coupled with innovative approaches earned friends and admirers as well as jealous adversaries. He and my mother-in-law (Harapriya, who died before him in 2009) have faced major tragedies in life, with untimely death of their two daughters – Neena in 1981, and Manorama (my wife) in 1990, and their eldest son's death in 2008. My father-in-law, Narasimha Kar, expired in August, 2013 at the age of 94.

My wife's younger sister, Neena was a very vivacious and wise girl, who got married to Brajendra Das (a UCO Bank Officer) and had two sons – Raja and Suja. Neena was very attached to her elder sister (my wife) and my daughters. She faced her cancer bravely and died at a very young age of twenty nine. Her children bore the brunt of this tragedy for years. They are settled now in life. Raja teaches journalism. Suja is a documentary film maker and a social activist, who has some of her mother's endearing qualities. My wife's brother, Prafulla, who became a Commerce lecturer in Kendrapara College, had an untimely death in 2008. Her two other brothers – Pramod and Pranab live at Cuttack with families.

My mother-in-law was a very hospitable and affectionate lady. My wife, Manorama, had inherited many of the qualities of her parents, particularly the magnanimity to a degree misunderstood by others. She genuinely loved the company of my parents, brothers and sisters, and took the burdens of family responsibility, including marriage of most of my younger sisters, with the least grudge or hesitation. Her uncompromising sense of honesty and frankness was the most valuable asset for me in my service career. She was doing some charity without publicity.

My friend, C.B. Satpathy had predicted in my second meeting with him at Delhi in September 1989 about my wife's health, which I did not take seriously, until two months later, when she was diagnosed with cancer of very advanced stage. I rushed to Shri Satpathy, who told that everything will be O.K. till April, 1990 and we should follow medical advice. As predicted, she was in complete remission till April 1990, but the recurrence of secondaries from May deteriorated her health since June 1990. She was very courageous and full of life. The doctors were surprised at her equanimity. She showed the least fear of death and never let any of our neighbours, friends and relatives know of her illness. I had to inform my in-laws in June, 1990. Shri C.B. Satpathy, who was transiting to Shirdi Sai path during this period, visited us a couple of times to pray for her and give solace. She was chanting, 'Om Namoh Shivaya', much of the time and told the doctors in my presence on 11 July 1990 that she "wanted to die tomorrow night or even tonight," and some palliative injection should be administered to her. She bade me farewell and breathed her last the same night. As per her last wish, we cremated her with the minimum ritual the next morning in the electric crematorium near the Yamuna river. As the sad news became known, our friends and relations were taken by surprise. Some of them had met her a few days or months earlier, but had no inkling of her illness! She had received them smilingly like she was her normal self. My life companion for close to 25 years was taken away prematurely by destiny.

My youngest brother-in-law, Pranab moved in with us during this trying period and was a huge support to us with his lively sense of humour.

I have three daughters – Bijayalaxmi (Bizi), Upali (Lizi) and Aptakami (Lita). They have all studied up to post graduate levels in India. Though the first two were brilliant students topping their classes or university examinations, I could not afford to send them abroad. The three daughters were brought up imbibing values of good human beings. We as parents never hankered for a son and were very happy with our daughters, whom we tried to give our best care, attention and love. The eldest, Bizee was a precocious child, very loving, garrulous and considerate to others, but very sensitive and straightforward in dealings. Like her mother, she is short-tempered, but soft at heart. She has stayed at all places of my posting in government service, and even after her marriage, I stay with her family in Delhi. Having got two gold medals in M.A. examination, as the University topper in Political Science, and the highest mark among post graduate humanities subjects, she completed M.Phil and Ph.D. with distinction and passed the UGC eligibility test. I have seen the last flicker of joy in the eyes of my wife on her bed, jumping out on hearing the news of her extraordinary success, a few days before her death.

Bizee was selected in 1993 as a permanent lecturer in Miranda House in Delhi University. She did not have the heart in civil services. She was destined for greater heights with her superb communication skill and super-sensitivity for critical social issues around women, children and the marginalised. She is loved and respected by her students for her teaching acumen, sincerity of purpose, easy access and mentoring through all these twenty years. Her research-cum-activism on gender issues (particularly the issues of adverse sex ratio at birth and trafficking) has won recognition nationally and globally, and she is invited to important fora in Government and Civil Society. I recollect the prediction of C.B. Satpathy to my wife in 1989 that she will be an excellent 'communicator'. A Bengali astrologer had predicted in 2000 that she will "command a submarine" of activism against the social malaise facing the nation in future, which she is very much into now.

She is now an Associate Professor, and has done consulting for WHO and UN. Her marriage to Rajesh Kumar (an officer of Indian Civil Accounts Service) from Patna was mooted around 1994, and took place on 20 April 1995. Rajesh's innovative initiatives have won recognition for him wherever he has worked – Labour Ministry, CBDT, CBEC, WHO, NRHM and Controller General of Accounts. His amiable temperament has won many admirers. Thanks to the sterling qualities of Rajesh, Bizee and their child, Akshara, I have continued to live with them since 1997 in Delhi. I do not impose my will on them and we respect each other's wishes and autonomy. They are fully supportive of my spiritual efforts and tolerant of my shortcomings.

My second daughter, Upali (Lizee) was a brilliant student throughout her school career and was trained as an Odissi dancer and tennis player. She got into Cuttack medical college in the first attempt, but was so badly affected by her mother's death in 1990 that she had trouble in clearing some papers in the first MBBS exam. I could not get her transferred to Delhi, and she passed her final MBBS and did her internship by the time I came back to Bhubaneshwar in end 1994. She got into State Government Health Service, and after her rural stints, got posted to Bhubaneshwar and stayed with me during 1995-97. She is married to Sunandan (Bubu) in June, 1998, and worked at Cuttack staying with her husband and in-laws until August, 2007, when she shifted to Delhi to attend to my serious illness. As predicted by C.B. Satpathy, she was selected for post-graduate study (DNB in Family Medicine) in early 2008, took study leave and stayed in Delhi. She has now passed the post graduate examination, and decided to resign the State Government job to join as a consultant in one of the Delhi hospitals. Her husband, Sunandan, has shifted his business to Delhi. They have a daughter Akanksha (Sakshi) and a son, Adarsh (Rishi) – both studying in schools in Delhi.

My youngest daughter, Aptakami (Lita) was still in school, when her mother died. It was a big blow for her and she became silent and withdrawn for quite some time. I got her admitted to St. Thomas school in Delhi. She was very attached to me – my loving 'Litki nani dhania' (as I used to call her affectionately). She studied in colleges in Delhi and Bhubaneshwar and after her graduation, she studied for MBA. She settled with a job in Delhi after her MBA in 1997. Her marriage with Sachin (her MBA classmate) from Jaipur took place in September, 1999, and they worked in Abu Dhabi (UAE) for a few years, before migrating to Auckland (New Zealand) where they worked and got citizenship. They came to Kuala Lumpur (Malaysia) in 2009 and moved to London in February, 2013. Sachin has become a Director in the firm 'Reckitt and Benckiser's corporate headquarters in London. Recently in April, 2015, Sachin has moved on transfer to Johannesburg in South Africa. They have one daughter, Khusi and a son, Ansh, who are in school. Lita is very meticulous in house-keeping and her culinary ability is of very high order. She did work in Abu Dhabi and New Zealand in some companies; but is not working now.

The death of my wife in July 1990 created a vacuum in our life. My three daughters bore the brunt of this tragedy, and the next few years were very challenging for them in their critical period of adolescence and early youth. That's why, I chose my path or rather a path was revealed to me by my Perfect Master, Shirdi Sai Baba to choose and adopt. With my preoccupation with the conduct of the 1991 Census, and the follow up data tabulation and reports, and preparation for the ICPD, 1994, I was trying to give whatever best I could to my daughters to settle down to normalcy. I left socialisation, club life and minimised my external commitments beyond my official duty. Even till date, we have ensured that the rules that my wife, Manorama had set for our home are followed. Her spirit guides us in keeping an open house, feeding all who come in with warmth and hospitality, treating our domestic help as equals and being generous and compassionate to the animals in our surroundings. Manorama was not acquainted with Shirdi Sai, but her way of life was in conformity with His teachings.

I have five grand children – three granddaughters and two grandsons from my three daughters. The eldest of them Akshara (Ashee) was studying in class XI in Sanskriti School in Delhi, with very high grades in examinations all these years. She is a budding talent in creative writings and social activism. Having seen her growing up since her birth, I am very fond of her. She calls me 'Nana' in the same way as my daughters call me. 'Nana' in Odisha is how father is addressed in some communities. In the Hindi belt, 'Nana' refers to maternal grandfather. So it is a common denominator of address by Ashee and her mother (my son-in-law, Rajesh is from Bihar).

I am the universal 'Nana' to all Rajesh's brothers, sisters, brothers-in-law, nephews and nieces. Ashee startled me in joy when as a child of a few months old, she crawl danced rhythmically to my tune on an infant rhyme "kukule kukule kukule cuckoo….." As she crawled on the floor, she would stop and gyrate her body rhythmically to this tune. This joyful experience remains etched in my memory, and I sometime sing this rhyme to her. She smiles, but does not dance anymore! As a precocious and intelligent child, she used to see TV channels on Discovery, animal world and nature, and Simbaa – the lion king was her favourite serial, as also the film on Shirdi Sai Baba. She would call 'Sai Baba' as 'Sai Mama' while attending my prayer and worship. My daughter Bizee became very worried when she did not stand and walk on time. Ashee was with me on my bed listening to her mother's words. She got up quietly near the big portrait of Sai Baba on the wall and started walking unaided, much to the joy of everyone.

Her poems, short stories and articles on environment protection for which she won prizes in inter-school competitions are very interesting. She acted as a child artist in a TV serial titled 'Atmajaa' on the issue of female foeticide. She also conceptualised and produced a short documentary on street children in Delhi, 'Dreaming in Delhi'. She has been part of the CAPF (Campaign against Pre-birth Elimination of Females) initiated by Bizee since 2002. She passed her CBSE school final examination in May, 2015 and is studying undergraduate liberal arts in New York University.

Ashee shares her birthday with the same zodiac sign and star as my wife, Manorama. As a teenager, she has became more reticent and serious and less loquacious, but she continues to be loving and caring towards me. She is very attached to her parents and is affectionate to her cousins. A poem written recently by Ashee on her grandmother (my wife) whom she has never seen is placed below:

I Think I Know You:

And I faintly miss what I never even knew
But I think I did through your pictures on the walls
And the black and white, now yellowed, vintage mysteries that I sometimes discover
Pressed inside old albums of an age years before my birth
I think I know you as my eyes trace your curiously familiar face
I try to take in all I can through pictures
I think I know those almond shaped eyes and those seemingly endless locks of black hair
Those carved collar bones, that slender waist
Even though I never heard
I think I know your story
Between my mother's muffled cries
When she weeps under night's cover thinking nobody is listening
Through enchanted chats with grandfather when he sits up animatedly and recounts
Every detail of those incidents of mischief and love
At that trice I know you, I feel like you see
And when darkness visits my cold desolate hours somehow I sense you guide me
And even though we never met in flesh I think I knew you
And even though I was cheated the chance to
I feel love for you
And I think I know you…
To Nani from Ashee

My granddaughter, Akanksha (Sakshi) from my second daughter is a lovely and affectionate child, who studied upto class II in Cuttack, and has been in Delhi since 2007. She is now studying in Bloom Public School, loves English and French language subjects, and has abiding interest in stitching, fashion clothes, drumming, basketball and reading comics. She has the ambition to be a fashion designer. She decorates the home and loves swimming and cycling, apart from socialising with her friends. She is very imaginative and loves partying with her friends. She is fond of English rock music and Hindi songs. She was very attached to her paternal grandmother at Cuttack. Whenever I was visiting Bhubaneshwar, she would visit with her parents the hotel where I was staying and thought that I had a palatial mansion.

My granddaughter from my youngest daughter is Muskan (Khushi). She has studied at Auckland, Kuala Lumpur and Reading (UK) all these years. She is very caring of her younger brother and parents, and is very attached to her paternal grandparents and me. In my two visits to Auckland, and two visits to Kuala Lumpur and the 2013 visit to England during the last few years, she spent time with me visiting children's park and swimming pools. She loves swimming, mathematics and English. She is fond of spicy Indian food as well as Chinese food. She plays many games including basketball and socialises with her friends. Like her mother, she is very spirited and active in home decoration and helps her mother in house work. She is studying in a residential school at Oxford.

My grandson from the second daughter is Adarsh Aryaman (Rishi) who is studying in Gyan Bharati School, Saket. He loves mathematics, music, basket ball and computer video games. He is attached to his grandfather, grandmother, father and cousin sisters. He likes her Bizee mausi's grace and caring nature. His life's ambition is to become a space engineer. He is very playful and lively.

The youngest of my grandsons from my youngest daughter is Ansh, who is a very loving child full of godly qualities and is a unique and special kid. He is a pure soul, who is born to make us egoless, humble, loving and caring. I call him 'Sai Ansh' – a part of Sai. He is a very special grandchild for me.

We used to employ one full time domestic help throughout my working career at different stations in Odisha and New Delhi. All the earlier domestic helps have been settled in permanent employments, mostly in Government jobs from Ghasi in SDO days to Gora in Odisha Census days. We were invariably treating them as members of our family and my wife was very concerned about their well-being and future. This tradition continued even after my wife's death. Ramesh got absorbed in Orissa Power Generation Corporation and Jaspal in the Departmental Canteen in the Central Government. After my retirement, Jamuna, who was sent by my mother-in-law in December 2002, continued to help my daughter and granddaughter for eight years. She settled down in marriage in 2010. We have been keeping a loving Labrador dog – Simba since October, 2006.

This is all that I recollect worth recording as I look back in time of my life's gross journey. I do not intend to stay nostalgic, contented or remorseful looking back and live the rest of my life on the laurels or follies of the past. Time has come now to look 'within' more and more and to find lasting peace and bliss in this inward journey. I feel like being born again as a child trying to learn and intuit in a spiritual world in the care of my Perfect Master – the eternal Shirdi Sai Baba.

Epilogue

Issues of concern while working in Government and Civil Society:

I thought I would present a summary of the broad issues of concern which I perceived based on my long half-a-century working career in Government and Civil Society. As I reminisced the selected events and presented them in different chapters in Part - I, I tried to give as unbiased and objective a picture as possible, with no intention of personal animosity or hurting others. The broad issues which have emerged could be grouped under eleven heads, namely,

Public Interest versus Private Interest

Integrity versus Corruption

Efficiency-Dynamism versus Dilatory bureaucracy

Transparency versus Secrecy

Political-Bureaucratic-Public Interface

Style of Generalist Management Leadership: What it entails?

Mindset of Sustainable and Balanced Development versus Quick-fix short-term Measures.

Mindset of Inter-sectoral Convergence and Delegation for Decentralised decision making versus one of authoritarian vertical centralism.

Mindset of Concern, Compassion and Empathy towards Equity ,Justice and Human Rights versus one of ramrod steel frame neutrality bereft of concern.

Mindset of Dialogue, Listening to other's viewpoints with patience versus one of imposing commands unilaterally.

Government-Civil Society Organisations Interface: Conflict versus Collaboration and Co-operation.

These eleven broad issues of concern have been treated and handled in varieties of management behavioural styles depending on situations, by different members of Indian Administrative Service in the past 60-70 years since Independence. The democratic institutions of governance have evolved over the years engendering opportunities, challenges, contradictions and contestations, both positive and negative. The Civil Society and People have also evolved in many directions with somewhat similar ethos. The eleven issues are inter-related in many ways.

By and large, ten issues (from item ii to xi) emanate from a leader's (political or bureaucratic) approach to the issue narrated as item(i) (Public Interest versus Private Interest). I have been a witness (and sometime part of the play) to the phenomenon of Ministers or senior bureaucrats succumbing to the lure of private interest masquerading as public interest. Integrity versus Corruption has largely been a bye-product of this syndrome, and vice versa. In some tenuous causal manner, efficiency versus bureaucratic dilatoriness, and other issues are also connected. There are, of course, exceptions of very honest and efficient officers having negative style of leadership or negative mindset on issues seven to eleven. They wanted to play safe by the rule book and did not take any risky or potentially risky initiative, much less to exhibit dynamism in the public interest.

One of the reasons for denigrating IAS has been the generalist management style of leadership lording over professional specialists and experts in authoritarian and judgmental way with snobbery and utter lack of appreciation and recognition of their worth and excellence. Worse is the behaviour vis-a-vis junior colleagues and subordinate staff.

In most cases, mentoring and guidance are non-existent or tardy. There are, of course, laudable exceptions. I have been witness to many cases in my service career both at the State Government and Government of India to prove this issue of concern.

Handling power hungry, eccentric or dishonest officers becomes a knotty issue. I have narrated a few cases of my encounter with this type of officers in the earlier chapters. Some of them are prone to flattery and are unethical in their dealings. They are invariably bullies who try to intimidate and demoralize the junior officers who do not fall in line. They go to the extent of harming them in their career record. Two Union Home Secretaries whom I was reporting as Registrar General and Census Commissioner in the early 1990s were trying to demoralize me. Similarly, there were two Chief Secretaries in the State Government trying to hoodwink me to fall into their unethical scheme of things. One Union Finance Secretary joined hand with the Finance Minister to dismantle the organization I was heading (India Investment Centre) without any consultation with me and I protested strongly with due justification. As the Government changed and both were out of power, the new Finance Secretary and the new Finance Minister (Yaswant Sinha) were convinced of retaining and strengthening the Centre. The earlier FM, Chidambaram took decision again in 2004 to wind up the Centre as soon as he became FM again. Had the Centre continued, the Government would have reaped rich dividends in terms of a powerful focal point for the investors.

As Union Family Welfare Secretary, I tried to manage four Health Ministers, of whom two worked for short duration. One of them was more often seen with a powerful lobby of doctors who were controlling Indian Medical Council and Indian Medical Association.

Another Minister Shri Shanmugham would take directions and advice from his regional party boss in all matters relating to financial transactions like purchase contracts. He did not heed the considered advice of the Financial Adviser, Purchase Committee and Secretary, and landed in trouble. The matter was brought to the notice of PMO and he was divested of the portfolio.

There were a few fixers, wheeler dealers and brokers who were hobnobbing with senior bureaucrats and Ministers in collusion with some business houses. Some of them were selecting senior bureaucrats for coveted or glamorous positions in Government, and even post-retirement assignments. They appeared to have some access to the powers that be, and were able to manage such assignments smoothly. I have referred to some cases in earlier chapters. I am not sure if this practice continues today.

On the issues of mindset, I have narrated a number of instances and discussed the examples of socio-demographic transition, sustainable development versus mega projects and gender dimensions in ample measure in the earlier chapters in Part - I. Some of the issues have been further discussed in the annexures towards the end of the book. For further appreciation, interested readers may refer to 'Advocacy Papers' published by Population Foundation of India in 2010. These papers go at great length on the above mentioned issues of Population, Development and Gender from a rights-based perspective.

The last issue related to Civil Society and its interface with Government. I have seen an inherent sense of mistrust, suspicion and allergy in many political and bureaucratic functionaries in Government, when it comes to the role, and contribution of Civil Society organizations or individuals in sharing ideas, design, planning, implementation or monitoring of Government or public programme. There is lack of transparency on both sides, and biased opinions without evidence or verification. Complementarity, cooperative collaboration and informed criticism from Civil Society reinforce and strengthen Government's effectiveness. The Civil Society's constructive role in governance, along with adherence to transparent financial and administrative rules of discipline and ethics is also the need of the hour.

Such balanced attitude and practice on both sides has worked wonders, as I have experienced working in various sectors in Government and in NGO-Civil Society activism. The understanding, appreciation and tolerance have to be mutual, but healthy. I have seen non-government funding agencies, foundations and NGOs (both international and national) in 'awe' of Government functionaries bordering on flattery in meetings, seminars and conferences, while denigrating or bashing them behind their back. They have a differential norm, when it comes to allowing them time in presentation in conferences. Such behavior with expectation of largesse or favour in return has been witnessed many a time. Very few players in Civil Society have the courage of conviction to call a spade a spade in front of Government functionaries. Government functionaries invariably get used to such flattery and red carpet treatment and are selective in returning favours.

The newly emerging concept of commercialisation in government contracts to NGOs for running or maintaining public systems or implementation of programmes has been distorting the very basis of not- for profit civil society institutions. PPP (Public Private Partnership) is essentially different from government NGO Civil society Partnership. The role of non-profit NGOs-CBOs is so different from private consultants or consultancy firms, and the same cannot be kept in the same scale or basket.

The syndrome of big international or national NGOs eating up small or medium Civil Society NGOs or Community based organizations has generated unfair practices. The big U.S. or U.K. donors or Foundations preferring NGOs or consultancy firms from their respective countries has resulted in some type of incestuous relationship to the detriment of Indian Civil Societies' evolution and growth.

The weapon of Foreign Contribution Registration Act being selectively wielded for silencing principled dissent and human rights based Civil Society activism is a worrisome development. Some Income Tax authorities create hurdles and dilatory tactics with expectation of bribes from genuine Civil Society Organisations. I am not at all suggesting Civil Society bodies violating the laws of the land. They need to be very transparent, disciplined and ethical in their work. Their dependence on Government and other donor grants and largesse must not entail their compromising their independence and basic principled stand on public issues they represent. People's or beneficiaries interest should in no case be subordinated or marginalized. They must adhere to integrity, quality, cost-effectiveness and sustainability in their operation of social development programme. They must subject their programmes to independent impact evaluation, scalability and sustainability. Both as a Government official during 1964-2002 and a civil society player post-2002, I have tried to play and propagate this rule of the game against odds.

As I have experienced, government's policy on civil society players (NGOs, CBOs, Academia-Research Community, Media, Social Activists) leaves much to be desired. Ad-hoclsm, patronage, collusion, indifference, attitude of mistrust and superiority (Government knows all) have bedevilled the sector more often, with the exception of a few officers for some period of time. We tried to build transparent Mother-NGO scheme in Family Welfare Department, which worked fairly well for some time.

Issues of concern to the Civil Society gelled in well in my psyche and heart, and I found most of these issues of people vital to nation building. Human rights and equity (specially gender) are more observed in breach in Government and big business scheme of things, and hence, are needed to be watched continuously by vigilante bodies in Civil Society. Judiciary and regulatory bodies need to be sensitized to gender equality and rights concerns within the overall gamut of constitutional, legal and global imperatives.

International covenants and agreements on human rights and gender concerns need to be complied with and implemented in letter and spirit, and powerful civil society watch-dogs need to be encouraged pro-actively by government.

Media has a very pro-active role in this regard. Unfortunately, media in most of the cases have been safeguarding particular private vested interests to the detriment of the wider public interest. I have been invited by print and electronic media while in senior positions in Government as well as during last thirteen years of my foray into civil society activism. I have tried to reflect the genuine concerns of public and civil society in the media at all time, to the best of my knowledge and ability.

Whether it was interpretation of socio-demographic transition and economic trends based on census or survey data, or on the issues of gender, sex-selective abortion, or on the distortion of public health and family planning issues in the mindset and hands of deviant and unethical players in Government, I have remained forthright, balanced and consistent in presenting to the media. I distinctly remember one instance of a television channel (NDTV) , which blacked out a portion of my comments on adverse family planning services, on the plea that it was not acceptable to the sponsor of the show!

I find Lok Sabha TV show on gender issues, where I or my activist daughter, Bijayalaxmi have been regularly invited, is doing more courageous and unbiased anchoring than most of the so-called powerful channels. The Women's Feature Service is also doing a fairly unbiased and objective media analysis of gender issues.

During my stint in Population Foundation of India (2002-2010), we had mounted big media advocacy and fellowship programme on the multifaceted issues of population and development including the serious social issue of sex-selective abortions. This went hand in hand with press briefings and special articles contributed by some of us to prominent newspapers. The Hindi language regional papers were very receptive and open. The only English national daily which was very receptive to our right-based and gender-sensitive approach was "The Hindu". I remember Mr. N. Ram (The Editor-in-chief) instructing his editorial team to publish my article on Population, on the occasion of the World Population Day, even when he was travelling abroad. Newspapers such as Times of India were less forthcoming and interested. They perhaps felt that such issues were not important!

These are some of my perceptions on the eleven broad issues of concern to society, as I journeyed in the course of my working career in Government and Civil Society for almost half-a-century (1964-2015). I felt all the while like walking the razor's edge, but in retrospect, feel quite satisfying and contented doing as per conscience.

Snippets of Some Unforgettable Meetings

In course of life's gross physical journey, I have met many people- some frequently, some not so frequently and some once or twice. Apart from close family relatives I have met and vibed with friends, work colleagues and elders at different points of time and at different locations. I have referred to some of them at appropriate places in earlier chapters. They were all important to me and continue to be so in my memory, even when I have not met some for years, and some have physically departed from this world. I am now presenting snippets of a few unforgettable meetings with three prominent personae (each in her or his own way) who are no more. They are Mother Teresa, Indira Gandhi and former Raja (King) of Tigiria-my birth place. The last person died in penury at the age of 94 in November, 2015.

I was working as District Collector, Puri during 1975-1976, the heady days of Emergency. I used to visit Leprosy Homes and other charitable institutions run by philanthropists like Sisters of Charity. Once, I got invited to a meeting in leprosy colony near Jamla on Bhubaneshwar- Khurda national highway. Mother Teresa was visiting this place. When I was introduced to her, she said that she was very glad to meet me and narrated about my compassionate help to rehabilitate the leprosy affected people. She blessed me. We shared the same dias at the public meeting. She spoke a few words which came from her heart. I remember the most unforgettable words she spoke on love and compassion to these people; "You love and love them so much until it hurts….."

As I have narrated earlier, I met Indira Gandhi first time in 1971, as Additional District Magistrate, Sambalpur, as her aircraft landed at an airstrip at Jharsuguda. I was introduced to her, and she smilingly asked me my batch year in IAS and a few questions about the district. She had come to address some election meetings.

Next I met her was at Konark Sun Temple, where she came in a helicopter in 1976 along with her two sons and daughters-in-law. I was receiving her as District Magistrate, Puri. She spent some time visiting the Sun Temple and had lunch at the local PWD Inspection Bungalow specially renovated for her visit. She was walking very fast on a mound and insisted on taking a shortcut down. I advised her against taking that slippery path; she stared at me and said angrily, "There must be a way down." When she found it futile to pursue her short cut route, she asked her doctor, who was down below "Doctor Sahab! Is there a way down from here?" As the Doctor said 'no', she took my advice and came down on the appropriate route thanking me profusely.

The third and last time I met her was in 1984, when she came to Odisha and left for Delhi in the evening. That was the day preceding her assassination. I received her at NuaPatna village (near Tigiria-my native place) as Divisional Commissioner. She was visiting this famous village of handloom weavers for an hour or so. She came in a chopper, and waved us to remain at a distance till the chopper comes to a grinding halt.

There was a rare glow in her face and she started mingling with the crowd of weavers' families – women and children – although the security was advising against it. She had already received threat to her life which she mentioned in the public meeting. She selected two sarees from the weavers and said that she would send back the cash from Delhi next day. The same evening, I was among the few protocol group to see her off at Bhubaneshwar airport. She thanked all of us. As she was going up the stairway, Chief Minister, J.B. Patnaik spoke to her that he would like to meet her in Delhi next week. I could overhear her replying that he (J.B. Patnaik) should check up her availability before coming. Saying so, she ran up the plane, waved us and got in....

Next morning, we heard she was no more......

The Raja of Tigiria (BrajarajBirbal), I knew from my childhood. He was the King of our area of 47 Sq. miles known as Tigiria State – the smallest feudatory princely State (Gadjat) in India during the British rule. I was too small a child to remember his coronation in 1943, but I faintly recollect the Rani (Queen) – a princess from Purulia (in West Bengal) coming in a colourful procession after his marriage to King's Palace, not far from our house.

The King had high regard for my father, who was the only allopathic doctor in Tigiria, and set up a hospital under his advice. I have already narrated about those days prior to Independence and merger in 1947 and 1948. The King was getting a paltry privy purse, and exhausted all his possessions including the Palace. He was an alcoholic and led a profligate life, separated from his wife and family. He came to stay in a dilapidated cottage in a small village close to my village. I met him once in 1996, when I was working as Principal Secretary, Energy in State Govt. and visiting my home. He remembered my father and recognized me. He offered me a cup of tea and talked of the epics of Ramayana and Mahabharata. He showed me some paintings he had sketched artistically on various themes of Ramayana and Mahabharata. I found him repentant for the follies he committed in life; but he was leading a life of solitude with contentment partaking of whatever food the villagers offered him. He was reluctant to accept some cash I gave. He told me that he is leading the life of a fakir with minimum needs. I persuaded him to accept the symbolic gift. He agreed on one condition – I should take some sketches as memento from the fakir. I accepted it with humility. As I was taking leave, he told me that he was proud of me as a fellow citizen of Tigiria for my achievement in life. I bade a tearful farewell to him, as he came nearer my car. He wrote me a beautiful postcard letter showing his gratitude, which I received a few days later at Bhubaneshwar.

That was the last time I met him. I wanted to meet him again during last few years when I was visiting my village to attend Shirdi Sai Temple annual day; but could not make it. My friend and well-wisher, Hemanta Babu (Hemanta Kumar Das) used to keep me informed of the Raja's condition from time to time. He went to meet the 94 years old ex-King in October, 2015, and told me that the Raja was addressing him as Nanda Babu.

In his death, he has been catapulted to his earlier glory of Kingship in many ways. Streams of visitors from the area paid their last respects, and obituary references were published in "Times of India" (From Prince to Pauper) and "The Economist" (King of Mud, King of Rain)" in exulted terms. In death, he was greater than life..... He was the last living King in India.

Apart from Indira Gandhi, I have met other stalwarts in national politics, in course of my official discussions in government service and civil society activism – such as Morarji Desai, Rajiv Gandhi, V.P. Singh, Chandrasekhar, Narsimha Rao, Deve Gowda, I.K. Gujral, Atal Bihari Vajpayee, L.K. Advani, Man Mohan Singh, S.B. Chavan, Narendra Modi and others. I have referred to some of them in earlier chapters....

Snippets of Some Other Eminent Persons

Some of the innovators and pace-setters in Civil Society whom I had the good fortune to meet have been mentioned in earlier chapters. I treasure the memory or association with Civil Society stalwarts like Dr. N.H. Antia, Dr.Ranjit Roy Choudhury and Ms.Vijee Srinivasan, who are no more in this world. Each of them has left distinct foot prints on the sands of time. Others who are working proactively with worthwhile innovations include Dr.Abhay and Rani Bang of Gadchiroli fame, Dr. H. Sudarshan from Karnataka, Dr. Thelma Narayan from Karnataka, and many more. Among the academic activists and scholars, I must mention my close association with Veena Majumdar (she is no more), Professor Amartya Sen (Nobel Laureate), and Professor Gita Sen (IIM, Bangalore). Among the special persons from the Bollywood, with whom I had unforgettable meetings off and on, are Shabana Azmi, Amol Palekar, Shatrughan Sinha, Shyam Benegal, Bhupen Hazarika (he is no more) and Kalpana Lazmi. We (in Health Ministry) had produced some of the best award winning feature films on the issues of population and development directed or acted by some of them. Shabana Azmi continues to remain in contact with me all these years through common threads of social and gender activism and she is on the governing council of CHETNA, which I have been chairing for almost of decade.

Shatrughan Sinha became the Union Health Minister shortly after my retirement from Government service in mid-2002, but he told me in the first meeting with him, where we shared the dais that he could not believe I had retired. He was fully convinced of the human rights – based and gender sensitive approach to population issues, and wrote to all state governments to withdraw restrictive two-child norm policies and other potentially coercive and authoritarian population control measures. He worked along with the National Human Rights Commission on these issues. Unfortunately, he had a very short stint as Minister, and was succeeded by Ministers such as Sushma Swaraj, Ambumani Ramadoss and Ghulam Nabi Azad, who were not on the same page (mindset) on the issue. All these Ministers believed in strong population control-family planning strategies and the first two were bolstered up with wrong advice rendered by a Health Secretary and a retired bureaucrat (T.V. Antony) who refused to understand the rights-based and gender sensitive approach.

Sushma Swaraj wanted to impose a uniform two-child norm restriction. Ambumoni was not interested in the issue. In collusion with the Secretary, he was taking many measures detrimental to rights-based public health and family planning. Ghulam Nabi Azad thought (guided by advice from USAID) that targeted family planning (female sterilization) had to be reimposed and that Sanjay Gandhi's Emergency measures of family planning were in the best interest of the nation. Luckily, he listened to saner advice and did not go too far. The present government are in ambivalence on the issue and leaving others (such as RSS and State Govts.) to take their stand. Family Planning, 2020 global campaign players need to be extremely circumspect on their new found enthusiasm.

As SDO, Parlakhemundi, visiting the highest mountain peak in Odisha exploring tourism potential

Attending a press conference on HIV/AIDS as Director, Population Foundation

Visiting a Lucknow Health Mela as Secretary, Government of India, Health Ministry

Visiting an Indian embassy abroad as Chairman, India Investment Centre

Attending International advisory committee of Pacard Foundation at Sanfrancisco

Visiting village school as 1981 Census Director

With my wife, Manorama

With three daughters, sons-in-law and grandchildren

Part - II
A Mystic Journey Begins

Sai Temple, Tigiria (Odisha)

(Constructed in 2010 by the Author as Trustee)

10

Entry into the Mystic World of Shirdi Sai

Way back in 1997, I was told by an astute Shirdi Sai devotee in Chhatarpur Sai temple in Delhi that the real challenge for a senior IAS officer like me at the pinnacle of service career is how to make a complete reversal of IAS to SAI! It brought laughter to people who were present. But I found, on reflection, that for me to be on the mystic Sai path or at Sai's service, I have to assiduously make such reversal real – the sooner, the better!

Even if I became a Shirdi Sai devotee from 1990, getting rid of heaps and heaps of Samskaras (Impressions, proclivities and tendencies) built over many past births and the years of wordily material life in the present birth of Rajasic and Tamasic natures inherent in the 'Samsar' of IAS with its outside attraction of power, position, ego, jealousy and comforts (even if some sattvic tendencies might be there, they are connected with the ego of self-righteousness) has been a herculean task. One has to make conscious and sincere effort to shed these attractions and come down to the reality of life. Our sincere devotion to Sadguru and His Grace and Compassion are absolutely essential in this process of reversal from IAS to SAI.

One has to surrender with all humility one's will to Sadguru, and be prepared to 'hang upside down' and enjoy the 'Bliss Supreme' as Sai Baba has narrated His experience with His Guru (Vide: 'In quest of Guru and God' in Shree Sai Satcharita, the life story of Shirdi Sai Baba by G.R. Dabholkar, translated in English by Gunaji). Enjoying the renewed life of in-volution (looking within) in bliss, with Shraddha (firm faith) and Saburi (patience with fortitude), and looking to the Sadguru with exclusive devotional emotion (Ananya Bhava) is possible when one hangs upside down, figuratively for the reversal of goal from IAS to SAI. That was perhaps the import of what the astute Sai devotee, C.B. Satpathy told me in a lighter vein in 1997!

I started the journey with SAI from 1990; but it has taken me almost two decades to come to a semblance of the mystic SAI consciousness within me. How deep I have looked 'within' (inward involution), and how much of ego of 'I', 'me' or 'mine' I have really shed, I can't say. But I now feel that most of the self-righteous narratives of this humble self's gross journey in life so far pale into insignificance compared to the elated experience of the inward journey in mystic Sai Consciousness.

The earlier spiritual experiences with Divine Life Society, Ramakrishna Mission, Brahma Kumaris, Sathya Sai Baba, Mahesh Yogi's Transcendental Meditation and Shwetambar Jain Saint of Ahmedabad were perhaps preparation for getting into the perfect spiritual journey with Shirdi Sai Baba around the age of fifty. C.B. Satpathy ushered me to Sai path. He used to take me to the Sai temple under construction at Chhatarpur (New Delhi) in the early 1990s, and I could get an inkling of his devotional service, which was attracting a large number of people. He told me then that all his search for and Sadhna after gods, goddesses and sidhis have ended, and was now concentrated in his Perfect Master, Shirdi Sai Baba. He advised me to attend collective prayers and Artis, read Sai Satcharita and visit Shirdi.

My first visit to Shirdi was in 1995 along with a friend, Gopal Patra, who accompanied me in a car provided by my friend D.P. Mishra from Mumbai. There was more of curiosity and questioning attitude even when I was unconsciously getting drawn to Baba. I had a brief glance at Swami Sivanesnand, the American lady devotee 'Om Sayee' at Shirdi. Suresh Panda (an IAS officer of Assam cadre), who was posted in Odisha on temporary deputation and was associated with the construction of Sai temple at Tankapani Road, Bhubaneshwar was also visiting Shirdi on the same day. On my return to Bhubaneshwar, I got associated with the Sai temple construction and the weekly prayer session in the house of Suresh. I read *Sai Satcharita* (English and Hindi versions) again and again, and got more drawn towards SAI. C.B. Satpathy's visits to Odisha afforded me the opportunity to understand Sai path with more clarity. When I came back to Delhi in April, 1997, I visited him in Moradabad and spent some days seeing his service of SAI in many ways – writing devotional poems, songs rendered to bhajans, inspiring devotees in temple constructions, writing books on the Perfect Master and giving unconventional prabachans – while doing his official work in Moradabad and Delhi with sincerity. He became a friend, philosopher and guide for me since then. He has spread Sai faith and way of life far and wide in India and abroad during the last twenty years. Though most of the Sai devotees call him 'Guruji', he does not approve of it. I had the pleasant opportunity to be with him in visits to many places in connection with the opening of Sai temples or other services, particularly during 1997-2002.

In 2002, C.B. Satpathy met some of us (Prof. J.P. Singh, his wife Urmil and me) at 'Sai ka Aangan' in Sushant Lok, Gurgaon, and told us that from then on, our 'ashram' life has started. He requested me to attempt reviews of books written on Sai for publication in the new English journal, 'Heritage of Shirdi Sai' every quarter. This gave me a chance to go through almost all books in English written on Sai Baba. But I did not know how to begin writing reviews on these books written by prominent authors like Narasimhaswami, Sai Sharan Anand, Dabholkar, C.B. Satpathy, Rigopoulas, Marianne Warren, Bharadwaja, Kamath and Kher. I dilly-dallied and in a dream vision, Sai Baba and His Ankit Santaan (chosen child) came to remind me. From the next day, I started writing reviews after reviews, followed by articles on many facets of Sai path including its organic link with Srimad Bhagavad Gita, Kabir and Sufism. Some of these articles were published in Sai journals.

When one goes to Shirdi alone and spends time there, one gets a unique feeling and experience, as it happened to me in 2002. The devotional emotion is something difficult to relate. The communion is direct and subtle, and is bristled with unalloyed wonder and bliss. You see Baba everywhere. The world becomes full of Sai consciousness.

When I went to Auckland (New Zealand) and Kuala Lumpur (Malaysia), I attended the gathering of Sai devotees in some centres and had pleasant interactions with them, some of whom are even from Islam or Christianity.

By the grace of Sai, I got the inspiration to write the nature of Sai phenomenon and Sai consciousness engulfing across religions, races and classes – the rich and the poor alike. The history of evolution of the phenomenon was prepared in a chronological time period. It has been published in 2011, titled *The Eternal Sai Phenomenon* by Sterling Publishers. I am reproducing below the relevant excerpts of the introductory summary on the experience:

"A true ardent devotee on the Sai path is intoxicated with the phenomenon when he surrenders completely to the Param Sadguru, who illuminates the path and guides him. He was, as it were, to move on a razor's edge, with care, discrimination, and caution. There is no place at all for exhibitions of one's pride, ego and one-upmanship, no place for religious or spiritual 'ism's or a feeling of superiority of one path by decrying other paths and other saints or masters. No jealousy, no greed and no quest for fame, honour or material gains. Sai phenomenon and Sai path is all-inclusive, tolerant, liberal, and humane, and full of compassion, love and service to all – Shraddha (unflinching faith, devotion and love) and Saburi (Patience with courage and fortitude) are the twin key characteristics of the SAI phenomenon. If one is resolutely on this path, the phenomenon manifests itself internally and externally and takes on others like a contagion......"

"Finally, the Sai phenomenon evolved out of the main mission of Sainath, the Param Sadguru, 'to draw out, train, help and evolve the human, souls to get rid of their karmas and 'Jivadasha....' (C.B. Satpathy, Sai Baba and other Perfect Masters). The effervescence of this phenomenon as we witness today is the handiwork of the same Sadguru..."

As I was engrossed mentally and emotionally preparing the chronological account of the SAI phenomenon, I was detected in August, 2007 with colon cancer spreading to liver as secondary, with metastases of advanced stage. Though shocking, I got mentally prepared for the worst. My daughters, sons-in-law and grandchildren were the most affected. Two major surgeries followed by intensive chemotherapy sessions over two years shattered me physically, but my intense emotional involvement with SAI's work kept me mentally steady. All through the last eight years (2007- 2015) of the episode of the dreaded cancer (emperor of all maladies) detection, treatment and remission, I realised the stark reality – the eternal truth beyond life and death. I experienced the Sadguru at every twist and turn of events unfolding. Devotional service and prayers of Sai devotees and well-wishers gave me strength, patience and fortitude to cross over this Prarabdha. If one considers this as a miracle, let it be so.

Two fall-outs of this episode of illness were the construction of a Sai temple at my native village, Tigiria in Odisha in 2010 and publication of my first book on Sai Baba in 2011. These I feel are the grace of the Sadguru and His compassion. I sold off my house at Bhubaneshwar, and decided to stay at Delhi with my eldest daughter's family.

As one looks deeper and deeper 'within', one gets more transcendental knowledge. Bhakti and Samarpan bhava smoothens the acquisition of this knowledge. This Sadhana is worth pursuing. Getting siddhis or even salvation should not be the motto of the Sadhak devotee. Bhakti is an end in itself. Siddhis and salvation may come automatically. The Ananya Bhakti bhav, which brings in peace of mind, balanced attitude, selflessness, delight in divine bliss and consciousness, leads ultimately to a state of 'Satchidananda' (Eternal Truth, Existence, Consciousness and Bliss). One expands one's consciousness in tune with the Cosmic Existence. One will deserve to be called the 'Amrutar Santaan' (the Child of Immortality).

'Looking back' metamorphoses into 'looking within'. One's perception in looking back sublimates and elevates, as one looks 'within'. None was your adversary, enemy or opponent. You forgive and forget with grace and accept everything as destiny. You become aware of your shortcomings and follies, but do not be either over self righteous or self pitying. Amend, what can be amended.

As you look 'within', you develop right awareness of the phenomena and objects of senses and mind, and simultaneously, of the subtle aspect of spiritualism, cosmology and devotional service to God and Sadguru. Your senses, mind and intellect get 'spiritualised' and elevated to Sai Consciousness. You feel unalloyed joy and bliss, which is ineffable. I quote from 'The Sufi Book of Life' authored by Neil Douglas – Klotz (Saadi Shakur Chisti) to re-enforce my experience of looking within:

"Real ecstasy is one of life's rare gifts. Sometimes – especially when we are not expecting or seeking it – one of life's peak experiences can transform our whole view of life in a radical way…" Rumi's expression of one such experience in a poem is soul-stirring:

"At dawn, the moon appeared and
swooped down from the sky to look at me.
Like a falcon hunting a meal, the moon grabbed me and away we went!
I looked for my self, but my self was gone:
In the moon, by grace my body became like soul
Luminous, I journeyed on as soul,
Until the mystery of Self and self was clear
Nine shimmering heavens mingled in that moon,
And the boundaries of my being disappeared in the sea."

This is the import of Sadguru guiding you to "hang in an upside down position"– in my case, from IAS mind, ego, sense and intellect to be liberated to Sai Consciousness or SAI (Sai Assisted Intuition).

The knowledge of Spirit or Consciousness is acquired in the process of looking within. Sadguru guides and directs you subtly, as you look up to Him like the young tortoise to the mother tortoise. The child is left on one side of the river, and the mother tortoise is on the other bank, but the glance of the mother is the food, security and solace to the child. Sadguru is like your mother, tending, caring and nurturing you at every stage. All you need to do is to concentrate on Him with 'Ananya bhakti' (exclusive devotion) and 'Saranagati' (complete surrender of will).

The training school of the Sadguru is unique – so different from the IAS Academy at Mussoorie. To quote Shirdi Sai Baba:

"He (Guru) put me into his school. How beautiful it was! There I forgot my parents, all my attachment was snapped and I was liberated easily. I thought that I should embrace him and keep staring at Him always. If his image was not fixed in my eyes, I would better be blind. Such was the school! My Guru became my all in all – my home, mother and father, everything. All my senses left their place and concentrated themselves in my eyes, and my sight was centred on him. My mind and intellect were silent and I had thus to keep quiet and bow to him in silence….." (Shree Sai Satcharita, Gunaji translated).

The path of supreme devotion, as revealed in Chapters 12 and 18 of Bhagavad Gita is acquired in the school of Sadguru. The mind and intellect get fixed in and affiliated with the Lord through the practice of Bhakti Yoga and the dedication of all activities to Him. This is complete surrender or sharanagati to God and Sadguru, and taking refuge in Him:

> *"Sarva dharman parityaje*
> *mamekam Sharanam Vraja"*
> (Renounce all other paths and seek refuge in Me alone)

> *Complete surrender in essence implies that "we should:*
> *do as God ordains us to do*
> *become like God and then interact in the world*
> *live in the world as God lived.*
> *adopt God's perspectives in life.*
> *just as God incarnate detached Himself from the body, try to do the same thing*
> *develop an attitude of selflessness.*
> *fulfil all duties as He did .*
> *and aid others, as He did to us….*
> *Lord's or Sadguru's essence and attributes are to be emulated and put into practice in one's life"*
> *(Exposition of Bhagavad Gita, Arpan Publication).*

Swami Sivananda, the founder of the Divine Life Society was my first introduction into the spiritual world way back during 1956-57, when I read about his life and teachings. I remember quoting him in a paper in my school final examination. The clarion call of Swami Vivekananda and Swami Sivananda of the Upanishadic doctrine: "Arise, awake and stop not till the goal is reached" had left a deep impression in my mind at that tender age. I have visited Rishikesh Ashram, read some of their literature and interacted with Swami Chidananda briefly in the 1980s through introduction from my friend and colleague in

Odisha IAS cadre, Sunil Patnaik (who has left IAS and become a Sanyasi by the name "Swami Nirliptananda" and lives in the Rishikesh Ashram). When I was attracted to Shirdi Sai Baba in the 1990s, I read the 'Foreword' written by Swami Sivananda in the book *Life of Sai Baba* authored by Sri Narasimha Swami in 1955, where he wrote that narrating, reading and listening to the sublime and mysterious Lilas of Sai Baba with "true bhav constitutes Sravana and Swadhyaya of a very high order. It comprises the supremely efficacious Sadhana for self-purification, spiritual awakening and God realisation." Swami Sivananda considered Sai Baba as "a Samarth Sadguru, who through His highest Para-vairagya and maha tyaga, made people realise the transitory nature of human life, and the worthlessness of earthly objects. He was really a Jivanmukta mahapurusha and a sage in Sahaj Samadhi. As such, he is in a state of oneness with God and thus, even after casting aside the outer physical form, Shri Sai Baba continues His sublime work of lokahita in an invisible form through His Abode at Shirdi!" (*Life of Sai Baba*, Narasimhaswami Part I, 1955).

As I look inwards, I find the subtle link among the Sadgurus, when it comes to taking devotees under their umbrella. I have not taken any formal initiation (Diksha) from any Guru. Once through the help of my friend, Debi Prasad Bagchi (IAS Odisha cadre colleague), I was on the verge of taking diksha from the senior most Swami of Ramakrishna Order, but it did not happen. I like to read books of Ramakrishna Mission and support their social service. In my book, *The Eternal Sai Phenomenon*, I intuitively brought in a subtle link between Ramakrishna Paramhansa and Shirdi Sai Baba. A swami from Karnataka and a Shwetambar Jain Muni from Gujarat predicted that I won't have formal diksha from a living Guru; but will accept a Sadguru of high order in my mind. In Odia Bhagavata, there is a stanza:

"Mana tohara nija Guru
Uddhava kete tu pacharu?"

(Your mind is your own Guru. Why are you, Uddhav, asking me again and again?)

This appears to have happened to me. Shirdi Sai Baba, who was in physical form till 1918, is accepted by my mind, intellect and will as my Sadguru or Perfect Master of spirituality. The bubbling up and effervescence of SAI phenomenon and consciousness in my mind, heart and consciousness is taking place in many ways, as it must be happening to thousands of His devotees spread all over the world. As I wrote articles and books on SAI, and as I am writing this memoir, I get deep within me the Sai Consciousness and derive indescribable joy and bliss. Sometimes, I get soaked in the elixir of devotional emotion (bhava) from which information and subtle knowledge sprout up in a natural flow of language, which becomes difficult to resist. There is no deliberate attempt for intellectualism or show of spiritual ego. I follow my intuition and pen as it comes from my inner being. This, I believe, is Sadguru's Leela and Grace.

My mind floats in the subtle and the unknown – in the subtle sky of Mind (Chittakash) and the subtle sky of deep meditation (Chidakash). Sadguru is seated in my Chidakash, guiding me through meditation. He then takes me into finer layers of consciousness. I yearn to be in this blissful state at all times! I wish to be lifted from my "Annamaya Kosh" (gross body with all senses, mind, intellect and ego) to the finer 'Pranamaya Kosh' 'Manamaya Kosha', 'Vigyanamaya Kosh' (intuition) and the finest, 'Anandamaya Kosh – the arena of eternal bliss.

Similar is the concept of 'Ascent' up the five 'khands' (stages in spiritual progress) described in 'Adi Granth' (Japji, 34-37, Adi Granth, pp-7-8), and the Sufi concept of "maqamat" – a condition of supreme wonder (Visamad), peace, consummate joy and perfect tranquillity

Two treatises containing important theories and truths (tattvas) of spiritualism, cosmogony and cosmology, which have influenced my state of mind and heart, as I look within, are *Gopyaru Agopya* (Odia) or *Srusti tattva anuchintanam* (Sanskrit) and *Shree Guru Bhagavat* (Odia in five volumes) published during 2010-2013. These are written in verse form by the ardent SAI devotee, C.B. Satpathy, based mostly on his intuitive vision and insight. I like to read these books again and again. I was so much mesmerised and elated that in the course of a few months, I wrote a rough transliteration verse by verse in English of all these treatises. I dared to attempt introductory reviews on these books, followed by a few thematic reviews, which have been published in the journal, *Heritage of Shirdi Sai* in successive issues during 2011-2013 and in my book, *The Eternal Sai Consciosness*, published in 2015. All this is done with unflinching devotion (Shraddha) and there is no pretence of intellectual analysis or ego trip on my part. The intention has been to share my joy and delight of the new found spiritual knowledge with the readers and devotees.

The treatise 'Gopyaru Agopya' (Unravelling the Mysteries of Creation) is a comprehensive treatment of the theories of creation, preservation and dissolution of the universe, living entities, energy and matter with all their ramifications. The nature of God, human beings, and the symbolic representation of God's power through gods, goddesses, celestials, rishis, Avatars and Sadguru have been presented with logical theories enunciated in ancient scriptures. The author has delved into the origin and development of the universe and all its components. Having very little knowledge of the Vedas, Upanishads and the literature on cosmology and cosmogony, I got a very clear, cogent and logical picture of the cosmic and spiritual science at one place. It takes you a few readings of the book with intensity, zeal and devotional emotion before you comprehend the theories. You find a reconciliation of various theories on the nature of God, Sagun-Sakar worship, and Sadhana, with Nirgun-Nirankar Worship and Sadhna, as well as many other apparently irreconcilable positions and stands in Hindu and other religions. One comes to know that Nirgun-

Nirakar Sadhana on Niranjan Jyoti is the best Sadhna, and that among the Sagun-Sakar Sadhana, 'Gayatri Sadhna' is the best.

The concepts of Time and Space continuum, the primordial cosmic theory (Adi tattva), divine skill and prowess (Kala Tattva), vital life-force (Praan tattva), cosmic sound and breath (Naad and Swara), cosmic principles of the Supreme God as 'Ishwar', Maya Shakti, Swarup Shakti, Yog Maya, Maha Maya, Buddhi tattva, Trigunas (three material attributes of nature), Som tattva (elixir of divine ecstasy), Prateek Brahm (symbolic God), Narayan tattva, Narad tattva, Rishi Devata and Avatar tattva, Guru tattva, Purushkar (the real God realised soul), Brahm Astaran (Blanket cover of God) and the relation of spiritual science with modern physical sciences have been elucidated with clarity, logicality and rationality laced with devotional emotion throughout.

The unique features of the treatise, as I have understood, consist of the following:

(i) Desymbolization and demystification of the cosmic symbols used in ancient scriptural literature.

(ii) Re-interpretation of cosmic concepts and principles of creation in the Vedas, Vedanta and Puranas in the light of modern knowledge and giving those a practical dimension.

(iii) Due recognition to the role of scientists and modern scientific discoveries and inventions, and their cosmic-spiritual role.

(iv) Indicative astrological-spiritual-intuitive predictions of the future of the world and mankind, and lessons for the mankind to be careful, but not to be unnecessarily panicky and frightened with superstitious beliefs or misconceptions.

This treatise to me is a priceless treasure for spiritual seekers, devotees and common readers. Once translated versions in other languages including English and Hindi are available, the knowledge on cosmology and spiritual science will be available to a wider readership.

I am reproducing an excerpt (my transliterated version) from 'Gopyaru Agopya' below:

"Just as the ant on a dry leaf
Moves about happily climbing the leaf
That leaf lies in a fish basket in a boat
That boat flouts on the surface of the sea
The sea is situated on earth's surface
The earth itself rotates and revolves round the sun
The Sun moves around the firmament of sky
The sky moves in the arena of the Universe.
And there are innumerable universes on the move in the firmament of space.
The mega universe (Maha Vishwa) swings in the womb of Void (Shoonya Garva)
From the ant to Maha Vishwa, all are in motion at all time.
All of these are active, but subject to change or metamorphosis.
All of these and the entire worldly life (Sansar) are connected with the Destiny's thread.
The mind, vision and imagination of the Ignorance bound 'Jiva' is limited.
The Jiva does not perceive the universe with his limited mind.
For the ant, that leaf is the only world.
It is terrified as the leaf shakes or moves.
The ant does not know that the leaf is lying in a basket in the boat
And that the boat swings on the sea waves.
The ant does not understand the import of the shaking of the leaf.
Due to ignorance, it gets terrified…
Same way, the human mind is always apprehensive
He is terrified without understanding the root cause.
By availing knowledge of the Absolute (Brahm Gnyan), one knows the root cause.
Through 'Sanjay's eyes' (third eye) or talented insight.
Taking the ephemeral or transitory as permanent or eternal,

He commits error everyday.
Committing mistakes, he suffers its outcome finally..."

(*Gopyaru Agopya*, Chapter 34, C.B. Satpathy).

The five volumes of 'Shree Guru Bhagavata' elaborate the Guru tattva in the context of macro-cosmic and divine plan of action of Creation, Sustenance, Dissolution and Re-creation of the Universe. One can perceive the macro role of the Sadguru within the macro expansive framework of spirituality and cosmogony. The mystic and subtle role of Sadguru in our life and death comes out loud and clear. The path of Guru Sadhana is delineated. The mystic subject of death is treated with clarity. The Guru-sishya relationship with all its ramifications has been brought out.

The more you read and recite the verses of this treatise, the more you get surcharged with and soaked in the devotional emotion (Bhakti bhav). In the words of Guru Nanak, you tend to be a 'Gurmukh' and cease to be a 'Manmukh'. The process of surrender of your will to Sadguru is smoothened and facilitated.

As one absorbs oneself in the hearing (Sravan) study (swaddhyay) and contemplation (manan) of books, like *Shree Sai Satcharita Gopyaru Agopya* and *Shree Guru Bhagavata*, one's vision and attention expands into the vast cosmos and wider humanity from the close restricted individualism, family and worldly happiness and fears. Issues and subjects, which were considered as priority, important and interesting in the material world (Sansar) so far (like name, fame, power, influence, companionship, wealth and family) become less important and interesting. One is attracted to the mystic and the esoteric in the wide expanse of universe. The intoxication of devotional love for Sadguru and God becomes predominant and over powering. This devotional service implies selfless service to the suffering humanity with all humility.

One looks at 'Destiny' as a combination of pre-destined events to happen as a result of one's 'Prarabdha' (Deha prarabdha and other prarabdhas) and 'Karmaphal' as well as one's disposition, attribute and new action incurred in this birth. The distinction appears to be very subtle. One can calculate in terms of 'debits' and 'credits' and the play of three 'Gunas' (natural attributive tendencies and dispositions of Sattwa, Rajas and Tamas). One has also to perceive the concept of 'Maya' (Illusory power) and the way we fall into the trap of 'Maya'.

As per Islamic tenets stated in the Holy Quran, God is one and sovereign and human being is God's vice regent on earth. The human being's conduct and action have to be in unison with God's sovereign command and he will be judged after life and will be disposed off accordingly.

As per the Sikh 'Adi Granth', the concepts of one God, His 'Sabad', Satguru, the nature of the unregenerate man, 'haumai; and the spiritual evolution (Ascent) with different steps (Khands) have been adduced within a logical framework.

The law of 'Karma' is explicitly affirmed in the 'Adi Granth'. Each individual should perform those deeds, which will, in accordance with the law of karma, bring the supreme reward – the eternal union with God. God's 'Hukam' (order) results in our birth and deaths, and 'Hukam' directs our path. 'Hukam' pervades all 'ahead and behind'. To quote the Adi Granth (an English translation):

> "He who meets the true Guru knows Him.
> He recognises the Divine Order and remains ever
> Obedient to the Will of God......"
>
> (Bilavalu Ast 2(7), Adi Granth, P- 832)

The practice of 'Nam Simaran' and sadhana brings in experience, which draws you nearer to God with 'Visamad' (immense awe and ecstasy) and death of the individual self.

The concept of transmigration of soul, cycles of birth, death and re-birth, the concept of liberation, the relation of soul and over soul have all been explained more comprehensively in Hindu Sanatan Dharma, giving out metaphysical and ethical messages for appropriate conduct in life. The concept of worldly life with the metaphor of 'Ashwatta', tree with roots upward and branches downwards in all directions, the balanced control of body (gross, subtle, astral, causal and super-causal), mind with its dispositions, intellect and conscience in the metaphor of chariot, charioteer, horses, reins and the road and the contrasting scenario of ego, pride, jealousy, avarice, passion, and anger on the one side and the scenario of compassion, pardon, kindness, peace and bliss on the other, leading to Truth, Consciousness and Bliss, are all parts of the grand spiritual evolution. The reconciliation of the paths of Karma Yoga, with Gnana Yoga and Bhakti Yoga, which is shown in Bhagawad Gita needs to be perceived. The nuances of 'Bhakti' (devotional service) with ramifications and outcome, the true import of 'Saranagati' (Complete surrender) and the concept of 'Grace' are very exhilarating subjects to be absorbed in.

As I look within, life and death take on a new meaning and purpose. No more bemoaning over losses, failures or lack of results. No more looking back and ruminating over the past worldly laurels or memories of joy or sadness. Whenever I remember the past events or associations now, it takes on a sublimated and positive delineation, which does not excite or disturb me, as it used to do earlier. I take more delight in the present, and look to the future with hope and serene positivity.

I would love to be immersed in 'Para Bhakti' (transcendental Devotion) and 'Raganurag Prem' (Supreme love) of Vraja Gopis and be part of 'Rasa Leela' of divine Love. I would like to do unceasing Bhajan and Ajapa Jaap. I would look forward to the day when everything looks 'Leelamaya' in the Bhajan or Jaap. To quote a ghazal of Mohammad Iqbal:

> *"Lets us sing every morning mantras sweet,*
> *Let every priest now on have love's surfeit*
> *Our songs of devotion now should give us strength and peace*
> *And in love alone should lie our final release"...*

(Mohammad Iqbal)

My life's story for the major part has been mostly one of a 'Conditioned life' (Maya Consciousness). The same consciousness needs to be attached to the Supreme Being and got situated in Sai Consciousness, with the Grace of Sai.

I pray to the Sadguru to open the divine eye of the devotees anointing the collyrium of pure knowledge and spirit of service to humanity, to handhold them at the time of death, protecting, guiding, drawing and attracting their vital breaths, as the sole companion at this critical time. My prayer to Sadguru is to give the jivatma solace and calmness, cutting off his attachment for the world and all memories of the life bygone. 'Death' is not the end of Life, but 'simply a pause, a comma in a continuing story" (to quote Swami Rama: Sacred Journey, Living purposefully and dying gracefully, HIHT, 1996)

Sometimes, I feel like Sufis singing and whirl-dancing in divine ecstasy. Sufi, Omar Khayyam's "wine and love' takes on the spiritual interpretation of 'divine elixir', as Swami Yogananda had explained it. I am charmed by reading the works of Sufi Jallalludin Rumi, Bulleh Shah, Kabir, Omar Khayyam and Guru Nanak, as much as reading 'Ram Charit Manas', 'Bhagavata Purana' 'Srimad Bhagawad Gita', Lord Kapila's Sankhya philosophy, Narad's Bhakti Sutra, Patanjali's Yoga Sutra, and last, but not the least, Shree Sai Satcharita. I am convinced of the role of my Sadguru in all this – blessing and guiding me at every step in the selection of Satsang, Swadhyaya of Shastras and charitable service.

From a routine mundane life of "Punah Punah Charvita Charvanam" (chewing the chewed) to a life of deriving new delight everyday or every moment is a slow and tenuous transition. As I look 'within' even while looking back or looking at the present or future, the perspective becomes ever new, and life appears to be more a part of the Cosmic life. I seek perfection 'within' in the divine plan of cosmic perfection. I quote the Upanishadic soul-elevating verse here:

"Poorna madah Poornamidam
Poornat Poorna Mudachyate,
Poornasya Poornamadaya
Poornameda Vasishyate....."

(Only Satchidananda-swarup Para Brahm – God – is Perfect. His active Creation of matter – this world is also Perfect. Only from the Perfect Brahm, this perfect world has emanated. When the fullness of the Perfect Brahm is taken out, what remains, however, is also Full and Perfect...).

(Brihad Aranyaka Upanishad, Chapter-5)

I remember this verse being recited often by a dear friend and colleague in IAS Odisha cadre, Vinod Jha (who is no more), way back in the 1980s and 1990s in a different context! As I try to comprehend this 'Poorna Swarup' now, I see the emanation of 'Prem Swarup' and I get the feeling of fullness of Love (Prem maya) by getting engrossed and merged in that 'Prem swarup' Paramatma.

To quote Swami Prabhupada:

"This life is a preparation for the next, and if we want to enjoy our transcendent senses, we have to purify ourselves to return home, back to God head...."

(Swami Prabhupada, Teachings of Lord Kapila, the Son of Devahuti 1995, P-56)

A Samarth Sadguru can deliver the devotee from 'Conditioned' life and soul to a life of Freedom and Light by removing the darkness of Ignorance and Avidya (Tamaso ma Jyotirgamoya).

Shirdi Sai Baba's interpretation of a verse from Bhagawad Gita (4.34) is relevant in this connection. He held the view that the Sadguru does not give you any fresh knowledge, as it is innate in you, but he removes the agnyana (ignorance). Sadguru helps us to cross the dark ocean of material world to attain another world, beyond this material nature, as narrated by Lord Krishna in Chapter – 15 (6) of the Gita:

"Na Tad bhasyate Suryo
Na Sasanko no pavakah
Yad gatva na nivartanti
Tad dhama paraman mama"

(That Abode of Mine is not illuminated by Sun or Moon, nor by electricity. One who reaches it never returns to the material world.)

One has to understand God to penetrate the material universe. That's why Sadguru helps you to understand God – the Absolute Truth – who is Eternal Existence, Consciousness and Bliss.

As I look within, I get more and more insight into many mystic subjects of transcendental nature. My perception may not, however, be very in-depth and comprehensive now. I have shared such perceptions in two books written by me titled, 'The Eternal Sai Phenomenon' (2011) and 'The Eternal Sai Consciousness' (2015). Excerpts from the latter book can be seen in Annexure VI.

Time has now come for me to stop writing my memoir and the quintessence of the present life. Let me pray to Sadguru to bestow on all happiness, well-being, bliss and a life shorn of sorrows and afflictions:

"Sarve bhavantu sukhinah
Sarve santu niramaya
Sarve bhadrani pashyantu
Ma kaschit dukhabhag bhavet.....
Om Shantih, Shantih, Shantih.....
(Peace be to all)

OM SAI NATHAY NAMOH.......
(Obeisance to Sadguru Shree Sai Nath)

Epilogue

Anubhav (Musings) in the morning of 1 January 2015

First morning in Delhi on return from a week's visit to Odisha carrying memories – gross and subtle, spiritual, emotive, cognitive and conative.

Heralding of the New Year – the seventy-third one in my present mortal life – with a mixed feeling of nostalgia, ennui, excitement and enchantment. Life's renewal is monotonous, mechanical and melancholic on one plane, and is refreshing, rewarding and reinvigorating on another. Both co-exist confronting you, as you inch closer towards departure from the mortal world. You try to balance yourself amidst the twists and turns of emotions, thoughts and desires, and breathe fresh air of optimism and options for the days to come.

I pay my silent obeisance to the Sun as He rises from the eastern horizon in a misty sky. I take a brisk walk in a circular path in the chilly weather for twenty minutes. The drooping flowers in multiple faded hues and shapes greet me with wry smiles, as they seem to be well past their youthful grandeur struck by adverse weather. There is mutual empathy and understanding. I sit down in the cabin for meditation over next half an hour – rising from disturbed thoughts to graduate into silence in deep mediation in the mystic realm of my Sadguru, Shirdi Sai Baba. The bliss comes with it in the emptiness of Mind, as I descend down to the gross world. I prepare my morning Darjeeling tea and sip it slowly, glancing at the newspapers.

My cellphone starts ringing – the formal wishing of Happy New Year from friends and relatives repeated with the same refrain year after year. I reciprocate and pray to Sadguru Sai for their well-being and happiness in the year that has arrived.

The years that have gone by seep my soul with impressions – positive and negative – gathered cumulatively of events, people and places, which memory has stored from the earliest days of childhood through adolescence, youth to the old age now. As the mind becomes less restless with some smattering of spiritual efforts, the negative impressions don more and more positive robes, perhaps, through sublimation and rationalization. Complete break with the past with all its impressionistic ramifications is not feasible at present. Maybe, it will happen someday – for better or for worse – either through spiritual sadhana or dementia.

Past relationships – gross or subtle – are the most difficult to forget, even if some of these are apparently or substantively obstructive of the path of spiritual sadhana or further evolution. The conflict and contradiction persist in varying degrees, from time to time. I can't gloss over it altogether or suppress it with firm determination. I narrate below six poems written by me, which reflect the conflict and contradiction.

Six Rare Moments of Musing in Life's Journey

1. *Enchanting Song*

The cuckoo sang the tune in riyaz
In the spring morn of first love.
The woods echoed the enchanting melody
Into the heart of the love-lorn bird.
The haunting music lingers on.
The ripple effect refuses to die.
It merges into the Time and Space of Eternity
As the cuckoo sang the tune in riyaz.....

2. *Scent of the First Monsoon Rain*

The scent of the fresh wet earth
Soaked in the first drops of monsoon rain
Reminds the love-lorn heart
Of the beloved's entreaty of reunion
Leaving all work half-way like Gopis in Vrindavan
The heart rushes to the eternal beloved
To dance in gay abandon
Forgetting the mores and rules of etiquette
As it smells the scent of the fresh wet earth...

3. *High Tide of Autumn's Fullmoon Night*

Many ages ago, on a fullmoon night of autumn
The two love birds in their unripe youth
Sailed the tottering boat on high tide of the tumultuous river
Singing the songs of innocence in euphoria
The round moon reflected in the face of the beloved
Weaving the delight of ecstatic dreams
The hearts were full – the dreams floated
Carrying the hearts in the high tide of the fullmoon night of autumn.

4. *Rare Moments of Togetherness*

When eyes meet eyes
And stay locked for eternity
In full concentration without a wink,
Wine of ecstasy in fullness
Is sipped in slow motion.
Feeling of oneness binds pair of eyes
Sharing rare moments of togetherness
As eyes sink into eyes.........

5. *Anguish & Yearning in Winter*

They are anguished hearts separated in the long march of winter

In the icy zone of despair and despondency
The yearning for the spring of hope and happiness sharpens.
The frost-bitten life refuses to yield.
They walk in emotive unison in dark slippery paths of snow showers.
Dreaming of the rare moments of togetherness in an uncertain future.
They hum the tunes of 'Gopi Geet' yearning for Krishna's reappearance
Will their heart's desire see the end of the long march of winter?

6. *Summer Evening of Musing*

On this hot dry summer evening of life's journey
We share long distance musing on reality check
What went wrong, what was right?
What is the Truth, what's the shadowy, 'make believe'?
Could we have re-engineered our destiny?
Could one re-play the long play gramophone record of 'ifs' and 'buts'?
We have traversed so far on our pre-destined paths.
Let's not try retrieving the irretrievable
Let's enjoy the cool air-conditioned comforts of spirituality
On this hot dry summer evening of life's journey.....

I pray to my Sadguru, Shirdi Sai, to guide me through the slippery path. I am aware of the imperfections of the past and uncertainties of the future, and of the clarion call of the present, here and now, to arise, awake and stop not till the goal is reached.

Annexure - I

A write up on Odisha Power Sector Reforms

Power sector in Odisha:
Past, Present and the way forward

B. C. Jena
Formerly:
Chairman, CESU, Member of OERC, CMD, GRIDCO,
Chairman, EREB (Now EPRC), MD OPGC

A Glimpse of the Past

Indian Electricity Act, 1910 dealt with the supply and use of electricity as well as rights and obligations of the private licensee. The subsequent enactment, i.e., Electricity Supply Act, 1948 dealt with statutory functions of Central Electricity Authority (CEA), State Electricity Boards (SEBs) and Generating Companies. One of the basic reasons for its enactment was expediting the process of rapid industrialization and rural electrification.

Under Supply Act 1948, State Electricity Boards were set up under the control of State Governments. Central Electricity Authority, Central Sector Units like NTPC, NHPC, NEEPCO, etc. were also established at the central level. PGCIL was formed at a much later date being an off-shoot of NTPC. REC and PFC were also formed under the Central Government for providing funding to the power sector.

1956 amendment to the said Act further increased the role of State Governments to exercise supervisory control over SEBs. Social and Welfare Objectives were of paramount importance. Stress was laid on rapid expansion of the infrastructure to meet the need for Industrial Development, which ultimately led the SEBs to incur huge losses in their operation, with widening gap between demand and supply associated with bad quality of supply.

The Supply Act 1948, Section 59 read with Section 63 made it mandatory on the part of the State Governments to ensure that SEBs post three percent RoR on their net fixed assets. Thus the state governments were saddled with payment of subsidy to fund the deficit due to inefficient operation of SEBs to comply with the above provisions of the Act.

In spite of phenomenal achievements, the SEBs became financially sick day by day. The reasons being Unrealistic Pricing Policy, Government Subsidy, Cross-subsiding by commercial and industrial consumers, Low Industrial consumption (leading to more loss and less revenue) due to more number of CPPs.

The result was that the mechanism of cross-subsidy became counter-productive and the SEBs started falling sick one by one.

After the adoption of the Industrial Policy Resolution in 1991, some amendments were made in the Supply Act, 1948 in an attempt to woo private participation in the power sector. The result was not up to expectations.

Schedule VII of the Constitution of India, contains three lists. The Parliament and the State Legislatures have the power to make laws on the subject matters contained in List I (Union List) and List II (State List) under Article 246(I) and (3) respectively of the Indian Constitution.

List III, Entry 38, both the Parliament and the State Legislatures have been empowered to make laws on the subject of 'Electricity', The Constitution has, however, given supremacy to Central Legislation, meaning thereby that if there is a direct conflict or inconsistency between a Central Act and the provisions of a State Legislation, then the law made by the Parliament shall prevail and the inconsistent provisions of the State Legislation shall be void (Article 254(1) of the Indian Constitution). However, if the aforesaid provision has received Presidential Assent, the State legislation can operate within the State [Article 254(2) of the Indian Constitution]. Despite such Presidential Assent, according to the Proviso to Article 254(2) of the Constitution of India, a provision of the State legislation would not sustain, if it is repealed, modified or amended by a subsequent Central Enactment.

Under such provisions of the Indian Constitution, Orissa Electricity Reforms Act 1995 was enacted with the Presidential Assent effective from 01.04.1995. The State Government of Odisha decided to unbundle the SEB through the Reforms Act 1995. Several other states like Andhra Pradesh, Haryana and Punjab followed suite in unbundling their states power sector.

Subsequently, Electricity Act 2003 was enacted from 10.06.2003 replacing existing three Acts, viz., Indian Electricity Act 1910, Electricity Supply Act 1948 and CERC Act 1998. The Electricity Act 2003 contained most of the provisions of Orissa Electricity Act 1995 through which Odisha pioneered power sector reforms in the country.

Present Scenario

The Odisha State Government undertook power sector reforms way back in 1995 and was the pioneering state to do so. Orissa Reforms Act 1995 was promulgated after the Presidential assent effective from 01.04. 1995. Consequently OSEB was unbundled creating GRIDCO and OHPC with GRIDCO being in charge of both transmission and distribution. OHPC took over all hydro power stations both under OSEB and the state Government. The only Thermal power station, i.e., TTPS under OSEB was sold to NTPC on 3 June 1995 at 356 Crores. OPGC functioned as an independent corporation in charge of the thermal power station in IB valley. From 01.04.1999 and 01.09.1999, the four distribution companies, which were hitherto operating as subsidiary companies of GRIDCO, were privatized by selling of 51 per cent of its shares through international competitive bidding. The shape of the power sector in the state after unbundling and privatization can be seen as below.

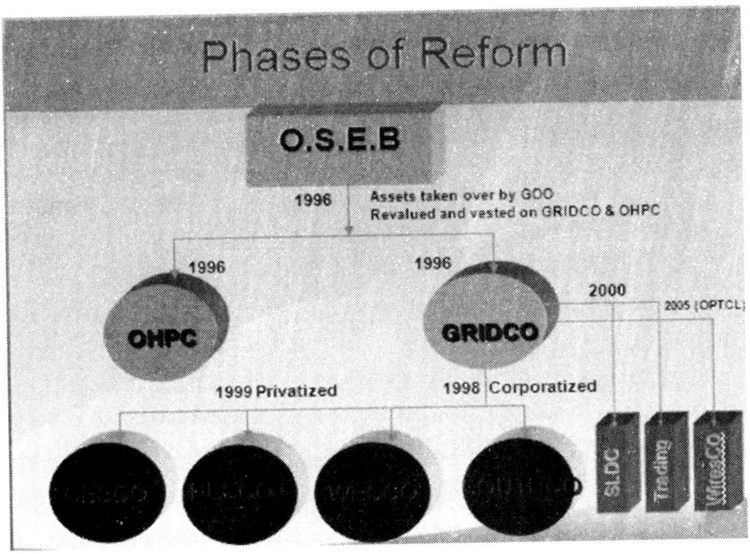

The following were the achievements due to reforms in the sector:

1. The State Government Subsidy, which was being paid to OSEB under provisions of section 59 read with section 63 of Electricity Supply Act 1948 was discontinued from 01.04.1995. The amount of saving on this account by the State Government to date may be around Rs. 25000 Crores.
2. Electricity duty collection increased from a meagre amount of Rs. 125 Crores to around Rs. 600 Crores.
3. The State Government received a cash of around Rs. 1150 crores by selling TTPS (356 crores), disinvestment of 49 per cent of OPGC share (603 crores) and 51 per cent

disinvestment of share of four distribution companies (170 crores).

4. The Aggregated Technical and Commercial (AT&C) loss has been reduced from 61 to 40 per cent.

However, the reforms in the sector did not produce the desired result due to the following reasons.

i. Billing and collection, particularly at the LT level, did not increase significantly, leaving a large gap in collection.
ii. Due to cash crunch, no capital expenditure work was taken up for network expansion to meet the consumer load growth.

The present AT&C loss level is around 40 per cent against a permissible limit of 15 per cent. In Odisha's context, each one per cent loss means around Rs. 95 crores of cash annually. So around Rs. 2400 crores are going down the drain annually because of deficiency in meter reading, billing and collection.

The following table will show all Odisha purchase and sale of energy in million units approved by the Commission for FY 2015-16.

	CESU	*NESCO*	*WESCO*	*SOUTHCO*	*ODISHA*
Purchase	8780.00	5250.00	7350.00	3420.00	24800.00
Sales					
EHT	1652.41	1548.83	1722.88	401.23	5325.36
HT	1120.16	394.87	1224.41	211.24	2950.68
LT	3988.03	2342.93	2962.11	1935.43	11228.49
Total Sales	6760.60	4286.63	5909.40	2547.90	19504.53

From the above table, it may be seen that LT sales is about 50-60 percent of the total sales. Billing and collection on the LT level is quite low as will be seen in the following table.

The Billing, Collection Efficiency and AT&C loss on the LT side as on 31.03.2014 are as below:

Name of the Distribution Company		*2013-14 (April-March)*			
	T & D Loss (%)	*Billing Efficiency (%)*	*Collection Efficiency (%)*	*AT & C Loss (%)*	*Realisation Per Unit (Rs.)*
CESU	45.7%	54.3%	84.8%	54.0%	2.14
WESCO	59%	41%	73%	70%	1.30
NESCO	51%	49%	51%	56%	1.74
SOUTHCO	46%	54%	46%	54%	1.85

(*Source:* OERC Tariff order for FY 2015-16)

It is interesting to note that the realization per unit on sale of LT power is much below the cost of procurement of power by DISCOMs from GRIDCO. The table below will clarify the situation.

Name of the DISCOMs	*Cost of Power purchase from GRIDCO. Paise/ Kwh*
CESU	285
NESCO	302
WESCO	310
SOUTHCO	200

The Discoms get most of their revenue from EHT and HT category of consumers, whose retail tariff is higher than the average cost of supply and their number is small, although smart metering arrangement like AMI has not been installed for these category of consumers to remotely monitor their drawal, variation of load, status of meter and load management during shortage of power. The table below will indicate the level of cross subsidy provided by these categories of consumers. The billing and collection efficiency for these loads are quite high to the tune of 95 per cent. Although billing and collection performance in LT is abnormally low, yet the average billing and collection efficiency of a distribution company looks good when seen in totality with the EHT and HT consumers.

Year	*Level of Voltage*	*Average cost of supply for the State as a whole (P/U)*	*Tariff P/U*	*Cross-Subsidy P/U*	*Percentage of Cross-subsidy above/below of cost of supply*
1	2	3	4	5=(4–3)	6= (5 / 3)
	EHT		572.03	83.22	17.03%
2015-16	HT	488.81	575.59	86.78	17.75%
	LT		396.53	-92.28	-18.88%

Details of category wise consumer strength as on 31.03.2014 and MU consumed.

	WESCO		*NESCO*		*SOUTHCO*		*CESU*	
	No. of Consumers	*MU Consumed*	*No. of Consumers*	*MU Consumed*	*No. of Consumers*	*MU Consumed*	*No. of Consumers*	*MU Consumed*
EHT	29	1646.4	36	1532	13	404	24	1618
HT	669	1161	392	440	260	181	1561	1000
LT	1030831	1393	1164741	1365	1253756	1135	1833090	2593
Total	1031529	4201	1165169	3337	1254029	1720	1834675	5211

Consumer and employee details Discom wise are as below:

	No. of employees as on 31.03.2015	*No. of Employees per thousand consumers as on 01.4.2015*	*Total No. of Consumers as on 01.4.2015 in lakhs*
WESCO	3628	3.60	1306080
NESCO	3116	2.67	831972
SOUTHCO	2793	2.28	636804
CESU	7427	3.96	2941192

GRIDCO purchases 25776.23 MU and sells 24810 MU to Discoms after a transmission loss of 3.75 percent, i.e., 966.23 MU.

Commission's Approval for GRIDCO's power purchase for FY 2015-16:

COMMISSION's APPROVAL			
Generators	*Energy (MU)*	*Total Rate (P/U)*	*Total cost (Rs. Cr.)*
Total Hydro	5881.74	80.44	473.13
OPGC	2838.27	210.85	598.45
TTPS (NTPC)	3177.32	251.50	799.10
IPPs	6636.35	220.84	1465.55
Total Small Hydro	320.00	368.00	117.76
Biomass Energy	125.00	575.60	71.95
Solar Energy	127.00	804.22	102.14
TOTAL STATE	20330.30	195.02	3964.86
Total Central Sector	5445.93	305.33	1662.82
TOTAL GRIDCO	25776.23	229.97	5927.81

As mentioned earlier, the AT&C loss is quite high leading to an alarming situation and needs to be corrected by improving Billing and Collection, which will automatically reduce AT&C loss. The methodology to be adopted is narrated in detail under the next heading.

The Way Forward

1. Distribution segment of the sector: Distribution segment is the most critical and vulnerable on which the sustainability of the entire power sector depends. It has to efficiently distribute the power and collect charges from beneficiaries with minimum permissible loss. Unfortunately, this sector is marred by inefficiency.

The following steps need to be taken as Mid Term measures with respect to Low Hanging fruit areas in the Distribution.

- Hundred per cent meter reading and billing to the consumers through smart metering system, completely eliminating human intervention, which is the main cause of ailment in the sector, is to be implemented. For this part, franchisee mode of operation as envisaged in Section-2(27) and 7th proviso to section 14 of the Electricity Act, 2003 (providing the legal framework for the licensee) to engage franchisee need to be adopted. The franchisee will bring the investment, fix the meters, maintain the system and take up meter reading and billing for a certain period. This will ensure no tampering and proper functioning of the meters. They need to be provided law and order support and government backing to realize the revenue not only for the utilities, but also for the government. In addition, there will be energy accounting and audit through the smart metering system, which will be provided in the feeder and the transformer. If implemented properly, it will produce miraculous results bringing down the loss level substantially in a short period of less than one year.

- States like West Bengal, Andhra Pradesh, Tamil Nadu, Gujarat and Maharashtra achieved substantial reduction of AT&C loss and maximization of revenue collection by providing law and order and political backing.
- Franchisee mode is suggested because it will spare the utility in appointing huge numbers of meter readers, bill collectors, supervisors, etc. which will make the system corrupt, inefficient and non-remunerative and, additionally, the franchisee will bring the required investment and maintain the system to the satisfaction of the utility. Even employing meter readers, bill collectors, etc. through contracting agencies will not solve the purpose as these have been tried in the past and have utterly failed.
- Energy Distribution, billing and collection is a very critical item, which should not be left only to the mercy of utility, because proper functioning of this part of the activity will ensure the sustainability of the entire sector, including transmission and generation, which otherwise will pose financial burden on the State Government, therefore, OERC oversight backed by government support can yield the desired result.
- Each utility has got several numbers of 33/11 KV substations with structures, power transformers, breakers

and other controlled devices along with a control room. These substations are manned round the clock on shift basis to ensure uninterrupted supply of power. Utilities have recruited technicians, linemen and supervisors for shift operation of the substations. The cost of these operations with recruited man power is quite high, whereas if these are contracted out, the cost can come down by 25 per cent. The contractor is responsible for the operation and maintenance of substations. To cut down cost and avoid recruitment of huge man power, this system should be adopted. This is already adopted in CESU and is functioning quite satisfactorily.

- High voltage distribution system (HVDS) needs to be adopted to eliminate LT overhead bare line conductors to ensure better voltage conditions and less interruption. REC has adopted the system in rural electrification under RGGVY scheme now renamed as Deendayal Upadhyaya Gram Jyoti Yojana. All LT lines should be through Aerial Bunched Conductors (ABC), which are basically insulated cables drawn overhead.
- Regular training of technical staffs at all levels is essential for knowledge update and hands on experience in operating and maintaining equipments, like transformers, breakers, switching devices, relays, meters, batteries, etc. This will add to their skill development also.
- At present, supervision of work by field visit is practically absent at all levels. This needs to be enforced to get first hand information of site conditions and will ensure proper execution of work in time.
- Field experience shows that through demand side management, the consumer drawal of power can be reduced by 25-30 per cent. This involves wide publicity and education of consumers. Kerala State distributed one crore CFL bulbs to consumers, replacing the incandescent lamps bringing down the peak demand by 100 MW.

- By distribution loss reduction and demand side management, the demand can be brought down at least by 50 per cent, which will save investment in capacity addition.
- Energy police stations have been setup in the state, the establishment cost of which is borne by the distribution companies. These stations are operating under the administrative control of respective district SPs. Most of the time, the personnel posted in energy police station are deployed by the district administration for law and order issues. The detection of theft of energy through a police squad headed by a technical officer is not being regularly done.

  Present position of Energy police stations in the state are as below:

Sl No.	*Name of DISCOM's*	*No. of EPS*	*Total Case Registered*	*Trial*
1	CESU	8	1849	NIL
2	WESCO	10	374	NIL
3	NESCO	6	495	NIL
4	SOUTH CO	10	551	NIL
	Total	34	3269	

  The present arrangement of Energy Police stations reporting to the district SPs is not yielding the desired result. This arrangement needs to be relooked at the State Government level.
- Special courts are to be setup under section 153 by the State Government for providing speedy trial of offences under section 135 to 40 under the Electricity Act 2003. Till now, such courts have not been established, as a result cases registered in energy police stations couldn't be tried in a regular manner. The existing courts are flooded with cases other than electricity and take the plea that electricity related offence cases need to be tried under special courts

as per the provision of law. However, to break the impasse, it is suggested that Hon'ble chief justice of Odisha High Court may be approached by the state government to issue necessary instructions to the trial courts to take up electricity cases at least one day in a week pending the establishment of special courts.

2. Transmission

- For evacuation of bulk power from generating station, 765 KV AC, 400 KV AC and 500 KV DC may be adopted.
- For sub-transmission 220 KV and 33 KV may be adopted. This means from 220 KV systems, the voltage will be stepped down to 33 KV. 33/0.4 distribution transformers will be connected to 33 KV overhead/UG lines for power supply to consumers. These arrangements will eliminate the construction of intermediate 132 KV lines, 11 KV lines, 132/33 KV sub-stations and 33/11 KV sub-stations, relieving the transmission company and distribution company maintaining the number of sub-stations and lines and also ROW problems. By this arrangement, power transmission capacity of the existing lines will increase by nine times. Existing 132 KV lines can be upgraded to 220 KV lines with suitable insulated cross arm arrangement without the construction of new lines (Andhra Pradesh has converted existing 132 KV lines to 220 KV by this method).
- There are several 220/132 KV, 132/33 KV substations under the transmission company, which is being operated on shift basis by employing directly recruited engineers/ diploma holders and technicians. This part of the activity can be contracted out at much cheaper cost without carrying the burden of recruiting a large number of personnel.

3. Mid Term measures with respect to low hanging fruit areas in the Thermal Power Generation Sector

- Reduction of coal combustion of coal fired thermal power plants through the implementation of efficiency improvement measures, like:

- Boiler Combustion Optimization
- Improvement of Mill Performance
- Improvement of Condenser Performance
- Improvement of Cooling Tower Performance
- Improvement of Regenerative Cycle
- Improvement of CHP operation to reduce coal loss during handling.
- Reduction of consumptive water through arresting leakages, blow down loss, etc.

• Reduction of Aux. Power Consumption of coal fired thermal power plants after conducting detailed **ENERGY AUDIT** through use of low specific energy consuming products/technology, like:

- New design of APH seals
- VFD drives
- Improved design of seals
- New design of Cooling Tower
- Modifications in the existing drive mechanism/use of energy efficient drives of Coal Handling plant, Ash handling plant equipment and BOP.
- Use of energy efficient lighting, air conditioners, chillers, etc.

• Reduction of Gaseous emission of coal fired thermal power plants through the use of hybrid technology like Solar.

The above list of measures are typically recommended for performance improvement of thermal power plants, since each Thermal Power plant will have its own technical issue, It is strongly recommended to conduct a GAP analysis of each thermal power plant operating in the state and then prepare a list of relevant recommendations for individual plants for performance improvement supported by a cost benefit analysis. The objective should not be limited to conduct the audit and submit the report, as being done in the present practice, rather ensuring that the recommendations are implemented and the end objective is achieved.

OPGC plant having Government of Odisha's interest is ideally suited to undertake such study and implementation. Further, the support from World Bank and USAID can be explored as they have a clear mandate to support such energy efficient and clean energy related activities.

4. Generation through Solar Power: Before discussing this issue, it is necessary to look at the present scenario of coal based thermal generation and its ramifications on the environment and climate. The State Government has signed MOU with IPPs for 39000 MW of which some plants have already come up. Additionally, the central and state PSUs like NTPC, OPGC, and OTPCL are mandated to set up coal based thermal power plants in the state. The total installed capacity of thermal power plants, both proposed and existing ones, will exceed 60000 MW by 2019. They will consume annually around 300 Million tonnes of coal, generate 150 million tonnes of ash and spew more than 450 million tonnes of CO_2 in the atmosphere. They will also consume two lakh cubic metre of water per hour, which may dry up most of our rivers, leading to serious problems on the availability of water for drinking purposes and agricultural production. As it is, river Brahmani is already dry and power plants like TTPS, NALCO and STPS Kaniha are facing water crisis during summer seasons when thermal generation has to be at its peak to meet the load demand. Such situation has arisen in Maharashtra state, where coal based thermal power plants in Nashik, Bhusawal, Parli and Paras with a total installed capacity of 3680 MW in Vidarbha and Marathwada region cause drought situation in many districts with no water stock left in two large dams of Jayakwadi and Ujali. This has also hit agricultural production and industry in Aurangabad area. Sixteen districts are currently facing drought situation. The same may get repeated in Odisha. Besides this, huge land will be needed for storing the ash generated by thermal power plants, as experience shows that much of the ash could not be utilized for other purposes, like road construction, brick making and cement plants, although the Government of India Forest and Environment Department notification dated 03.11.2009 stipulates 100 per cent utilization of generated ash within a period of three years for new plants and in a period of five years for old plants within 2014.

It may please be noted that most of the power generated will be meeting the requirements of other States at the environmental risk of Odisha, although Odisha's own requirement of power by end of 2031-32 will be 11280 MW as assessed by Central Electricity Authority. The present peak demand of Odisha is around 4000 MW.

We cannot do away with coal based thermal generation as at present they meet 60 percent of the total energy demand across the country. However, further generation through coal based plants needs tc be curtailed and improvement in technology of the existing plants should be urgently taken up to reduce coal consumption.

In Odisha's context, the alternative option will be to locate these proposed power plants near the coast where sea water can be used by the plants. Secondly, the generated ash can be exported out to Middle East countries to meet their huge requirement of construction.

Existing captive power plants including that of NALCO should be replaced by super critical large capacity plants from which each industrial consumer can avail its share as per share holding pattern. This will eliminate atmospheric pollution to a great extent.

Urgent steps need to be taken to explore the possibilities of generating power from renewable sources of energy like wind, biogas, bagsse, etc. The generation of power through Nuclear Energy option needs to be seriously considered. However, the generation of power through solar energy is going to be the mainstay in the years to come. Countries like USA, Spain, South Africa, UAE, China, Japan, Germany and Australia have gone in a big way for solar generation, adopting CSP with Molten Salt Technology to ensure 24 hrs power availability.

Water reservoirs of hydro power stations, other water bodies like lakes, embankment slopes, mine overburden areas, unused land allotted to industries are excellent sites for solar generation, the cost of which will be less as there are no land acquisition issues.

Roof top Solar PV is now catching up the interest of consumers in the towns and urban areas. There will be no issue of right way and the peak energy demand can substantially be reduced if a large number of consumers opt for such generations.

At present 30 per cent central subsidy is available. But that is not sufficient for a consumer to service the debt to be incurred to purchase and install the equipments. Three options as mentioned below may be considered to make the scheme viable.

- Ten per cent additional state subsidy as is being given in Gujarat.
- Incentive for not purchasing the generated power by GRIDCO and no transmission and distribution loss. This has to be considered by OERC.
- Arranging loans for the consumer at a concessional rate of 4-5 per cent.
- Accelerated Depreciation benefit and Income tax benefit to be extended to individual householders similar to corporate entities.

5. Skill Development, Capacity Building and Training

- All freshers and working professionals should compulsorily undergo training on Power plants for knowledge update of new technologies and learning best practices of operation, as envisaged in the recent circular issued by CEA. This training has been made mandatory by CEA, ministry of power, Government of India.
- Non-availability of skilled workmen, engineers with knowledge of operating power plants is a very big constraint in the construction, operation and maintenance of power plants of all categories.

- The best solution will be to provide a curriculum on power plant technology as prescribed by CEA integrated with the core undergraduate/Diploma curriculum in Mech./Elec./ Instrumentation. This will give immense employment benefit to the students, as they will be having additional professional training on power plant by the time they complete the undergraduate/diploma course.
- CEA recognized training institutes can be asked to take up these classes, which will necessarily include on the job training including operation through simulators.
- The training fees for each student can be met as a stipend by the State Government/GOI.
- Mid-Career training of technical personnel has to be introduced and made compulsory to update knowledge and exposure to new technology. This should be a part of service condition of employment.
- Government should ask the industries to open ITIs exclusively on power sector to develop power sector specific trained technicians; instead of going for general ITIs.

There are several issues facing the power sector. However, this note has covered only critical issues, which need to be addressed for commercial viability of the sector and also address serious environmental issues arising out of indiscriminate coal based thermal generation.

Annexure - II

Population Problem: Myths and Realities

I Introduction: Why this Topic?

Myths and misconceptions abound on population issue, globally and more so in India. An elitist, middle class mentality of self-righteousness and blame game is responsible for this. It becomes a convenient alibi or plea for ascribing failings in government implementation on the socio-economic development front. The reality of the 'Population' issue is either not 'internalized' in mind or is deliberately distorted or glossed over. The call for authoritarian 'Population Control' becomes louder and louder, resulting in 'quick- fix' solutions, which become counter-productive, anti-poor, anti-women with long term adversity. Personally, I have been a witness to and part of the story of Population and Development saga over the last half a century of working in Government and Civil Society. That's why, I thought of sharing some ideas through today's oration.

II Common Myths and Their Reality Counterparts

Let me, at the outset flag off major myths/misconceptions along with the corresponding realities at the conceptual front. These are:Firstly, the population growth saga – the myth of a "Population Explosion". The last three decades of steady decline of population growth in terms of annual/decadal growth rate, birth rate and Total Fertility Rate in India explodes this common myth. This is across all population groups – rural or urban, poor, middle class or rich. This is the reality.

The second myth connected with the first one relates to continuous and uncontrolled increase of the population size – from 36 crores in 1951 to about 126 crores by now. The Reality is the "Population Momentum" factor, which explains the demographic transition process. The population size 'phobia' needs to be set at rest by perceiving the reality.

Third, the myth of the large population as the real reason for high levels of poverty, low per capital income, slow economic growth, shortfall or depletion of resources is not borne by reality. It is the skewed distribution system coupled with lack of equitable access to health, education, nutrition and well-being as well as the pattern of consumption, which is the main reason for the phenomena.Similar is the myth of ascribing environmental pollution, global warming or ecological disaster at the door of the population (largely of the poor). The reality is the other way – the pattern of exploitation or consumption by a few and lack of access to the minimum resources and social development by the poor.

These conceptual myths lead to misconceptions and deeply biased mind-set around the population problem, bordering on hatred and phobia against the sections of population, who are perceived as reproducing irresponsibly and in an uncontrolled manner. This further leads to 'knee-jerk' reactions and devising of 'quick-fix' by hook or by crook solutions for Population Control, which turns out to be 'counter-productive', unfriendly and coercive in the end.

This has been more or less the dominant perspective in the story of 'Population problem' globally as well as in India for the major part of the 20th century. That takes us to the third part of my today's oration, which is the Genesis and Evolution of the problem.

III Genesis and Evolution of the Problem and Population Control Efforts Globally and in India

The stand alone and focussed "Population Control" policy-programme mind-set based on 'myths' as discussed earlier leading to unintended negative and adverse consequences has its genesis or foundation seed in Malthus's super classic written in 1798 titled, "An Essay on the Principle of Population". Ricardo, the father of modern Economics, brought Malthus's population theory into that structure in such a simplified version as to promote a misconception on the Essay's actual content. Malthus's central ideas have been often misunderstood even by professional demographers and neo- Malthusians.

Institutionalisation of linkages internationally among economics, eugenics, demography and population control in the last 100 years or so ensued in 1900, with the first in a series of international population conferences. The Birth Control movement led by Margaret Sanger after World War I, with women's welfare at heart, had to make peace with the gathering force of eugenics around the issue of population control. The phobia of "Yellow peril", "surplus coloured men", smacking of radical prejudices of the whites, became the predominant concern behind pushing birth control efforts. Apart from demographers, Carr Saunders, Cox and Blacker in the 1920s, economists like Harold Wright warned that population trends "may, if they are not modified, destroy western civilisation in a few years", and urged for "a world policy in regard to population problems". (Wright, 1923). The phobia of 'yellow', 'brown' and 'black' peril in the minds of the whites in that period was a 'myth' as against the reality that the population growth rates in Japan, India and other countries in Asia and Africa were then less compared to those in the countries of Europe and the broad-based public health campaigns had barely begun in these countries with yellow, brown and black population. This was the background of India becoming the focus of international birth control efforts from the 1920s and 30s.

The tendency to go for a coercive policy of compulsory birth control persisted from 1927 World Population Conference at Geneva through similar discussions in the decades of 1930s, 40s, 50s, 60s and 70s. Such a tendency smacks of an alarmist, racialist and over-simplistic view of a complex personal and societal issue, which needs to be perceived with the utmost circumspection, care, empathy and sensitivity.

In the sixth international Neo-Malthusian and Birth Control Conference held in New York in 1925, an Indian delegate, Taraknath Das, countered the "Yellow peril" with evidence of "White peril" and emphasized that birth control has to be only a part of a broader programme that aimed at removing poverty, poor health and ignorance, that were the root causes of India's population problem. He emphasised a perspective building of health and social development to afford greater freedom to women and greater opportunity for real education. Louis Dublin, a demographer, warned against disregard of the permanent interest of the state by promoting birth control, and cautioned on the issue of contraceptive safety and reliability. Thus, the issue of fertility control remained unresolved: "How to be controlled, by whom, and for what purposes."The conflict between the myths and realities around population issue was evident in India from the 1930s onwards. The obsession with myths found in the 1930s publications by P.K. Wattal, B.T. Ranadive and Radhakamal Mukherjee influenced the mindset of authoritarianism of the higher elites and middle class on the population issue over next half-a-century. Radhakamal Mukherjee, who convened the first India Population Conference in Lucknow in 1936, headed the sub-committee on Population of the "National Planning Committee" of the Indian National Congress in the 1930s. On the other hand, Mahatma Gandhi's vision of population problem was more realistic. He advocated gender justice and women's empowerment as a priority along with 'Gram Swaraj' towards achieving smaller, but healthier families, as against stand-alone artificial birth control, in his encounter with Margaret Sanger and How-Martyn. Nehru's ideas on population control were based on liberalism and creation of an enabling environment for choices.

The national programme of family planning in India coincided with the onset of the Five Year Plan in 1952, which emphasized 'Family Planning' to the extent necessary for reducing birth rates to stabilise the population at a level consistent with the requirement of national economy. A clinic-based approach with equal emphasis on natural methods, such as rhythm as well as some contraceptives were adopted cautiously, along with awareness building and research on new contraceptives and their acceptability. A Family Planning Research and Programme Committee was constituted, which in 1953 took quite a comprehensive and broad view of population programme. The Committee emphasized on the growth of family welfare from the social, economic and cultural points of view, and recommended 'Family Planning Centres' with role on sex education, marriage counselling, marriage hygiene, birth spacing and other measures including infertility as necessary to promote the welfare of the families.

Paying a lip service to the rational and sane advice of the Committee in 1953, Government adopted disjointed, verticalised, top-down contraceptive programmes with targets, particularly from 1966. Financial incentives were introduced for acceptors. Although the programme was integrated with MCH during the 4th Plan and with Health and Nutrition in the 5th Plan, the primary objective was to achieve targets of contraceptives, particularly sterilization and IUCD. The myth-based strategy reached a crescendo during the Emergency, with compulsory and coercive nature, making it unpopular.

Around the same period in China (1950s-1970s), the Mao Zedong's Government looked at Population basically as an asset, and took many revolutionary measures of social development, which brought in equitable access to basic education, health and assets/income. The concept of Family

Planning Services that China followed was more in tune with the recommendations of the Indian F.P. Research and Programme Committee. Moreover, China went in for a Communist party cadre-led localised community approach, and was more alert to the equitable distribution of services, despite overall shortages and deficiencies. Such a style of governance brought quick results in most of the indicators of social development including women's status; and fertility rate had come down sharply by the 1970s. The perceptions of the families and that of the state converged more or less, when it came to the acceptance of family planning services. However, the mindset of Chinese leaders post-Mao changed into a neo-Malthusian one leading to the imposition of a 'One Child Policy' in 1979 in the wake of liberalisation and with contagion of Western education. This Policy has been counter-productive leading to many social and family problems, including adverse Sex Ratio at Birth. The Population Myths overtook the Reality, which they had perceived rightly in earlier two decades.

Demographers and eugenics birth control proponents in the USA and the West shifted their attention in the 1950s and 60s from the poor and ethnic minorities in their own societies and countries to the population growth in underdeveloped countries. The Cold War bolstered by the study and interpretation of demographic trends engendered the fear of 'Population Bomb' and 'Population Explosion' on the same pedestal of anxiety as the nuclear war. Doomsdayers, like Paul Ehrlich cemented international fears of Population Explosion in India and China, with threat to the security of USA. Prof. Brand's report on the world population problem influenced the State Department of the US Government's report on the same subject in July, 1959.

The Neo-Malthusian twist during the 1959 International Population Problem Conference came loud and clear in support of the myths surrounding the issue, when it was argued that Population was a cause of poverty, rather than a result of poverty. The argument was based on the assumption that underdeveloped countries and particularly, the poor and lower class communities therein are "to blame for their unfettered fertility, which leads to their poverty. Their fertility, therefore, must be controlled to ensure greater economic prosperity for the families of the poor, for the nations, and for the world as a whole, since the large poor population in the Third world are considered a drain on the world's resources".

"The Club of Rome" Report, 1972 (Limits to Growth) and even the "Global 2000 Report to the President, 1980" in the USA continued the Neo-Malthusian stance.

More rational and sensitive scholars and thinkers, like the Belgian sociologist, E. Dupreel and Julian Simon dismissed these alarmist reports, and the arguments of the Neo-Malthusian economists. Simon remarked in 1981 that "people with a lot of education tend to lack respect for the capacity of the people, who are poor and have had less education, to cope, and may therefore worry that they won't be able to handle their problems in their parts of the world."

The drive to reduce population growth and size through stand alone Family Planning initiatives in India was, to quote Hollan: "A response to increasing pressure by international lending or donor organisations (World Bank, USAID and Ford Foundation) to step up population control programmes as a condition for economic development." Its impact on the experience of the poor and marginalised has, more often than not, been negative, inhuman and disastrous. The cause was discredited for various reasons, such as failure of early fertility limitation, coercive measures, prediction or prophecy of gloom and doom of global famine not coming true, and internal divisions and external oppositions in the family planning coalition from new and powerful constituencies like feminists, human rights advocates and environmentalists.

The global perspectives started changing slowly as was noticed in Bucharest and Mexico Population Conferences in 1974 and 1984 respectively, as family size grew smaller leading to population decline in some regions and below replacement level of fertility in some other regions. The languages of Population Control got slowly muted towards 'Population and Development', 'Population Stabilisation', 'Gender Equity, Equality and Justice', 'Quality of Care', 'Reproductive Rights' and the primacy of women's health and rights. The paradigm shift became prominent with ICPD, 1994, which provided a realistic dimension to the resolution of Population problem in all stages of demographic transition.

IV Dawn of the Era of Realism and the Continuing Ambivalences

Globally, two landmark breakthroughs on health rights and population development paradigm brought in the era of realism, namely, the Alma Ata Declaration of 1978 and the ICPD Programme of Action, 1994. The comprehensive Primary Health Care approach evolved at Alma Ata envisaged the notion of equitable Health access for all, which was "a potentially revolutionary concept that looked far beyond the customary boundaries of curative and preventive medicine and tried to address the underlying social causes of poverty, hunger and poor health." (Abou Zahr C, 1999). 'Primary Health Care' guided by five principles of equitable distribution, community involvement, focus on prevention, appropriate technology and a multi-sectoral approach was to be grounded in a broad theory of development that rejected economic modernization as the only path to well-being, and placed 'good health' firmly at the centre of economic growth, equity and productive nexus.

The 1994 ICPD Programme of Action similarly challenged the established way of doing things on Population and Development, and the new paradigm reflected a conceptual linkage of the discourse on human rights with that of health and family planning. It envisaged a radical shift away from technology driven top-down approaches to population and development programmes planned from the grassroots community level upwards. Family planning service was to be situated within comprehensive Reproductive Health and Rights, further integrated within the ambit of Comprehensive Primary Health Care in the overall socio-economic Development. Gender equity, equality, Reproductive Rights and choices and women's empowerment, along with 'Quality of Care' rather than demographic targets per se were to be set as the new goals of Population and Development. There was a distinct shift in global policy focus from 'Population Control' rationale and the associated myths surrounding that.

The Government of India reflected the philosophy of Alma Ata Declaration in the National Health Policy, 1983 and that of ICPD POA in the National Population Policy, 2000. Besides, contraceptive- specific targets were already abolished by 1997, along with the introduction of the 'Target-Free Approach', Community Needs Assessment Approach and a Reproductive and Child Health programme, which was to be need-based, client-centred and with a 'life-cycle' approach built in. The NPP, 2000 set fourteen socio- demographic goals, twelve strategic themes with inter-sectoral convergence and a 100+ point Action Plan to be pursued as a national movement. There was no place for demographic only goals nor was there the language of population phobia, population control, stand-alone family planning or incentives/disincentives. The vital discourses of the new policy, such as (i) Participatory Community based planning and Monitoring, (ii) Target-free, (iii) Life cycle and (iv) Social Health are, to quote Hollan: "not merely top-down instruments of propaganda, but, in fact have long been brewing at the local level, as evidenced by the local critiques of earlier policies pursued since the 1960s."

Therefore, regardless of whether or not the Governments are now capable of and committed to implementing a policy that reflects a fundamental reorientation towards women's health and Reproductive Rights, "the rhetoric of the policy resonates the local concerns of the women who are the recipients of health services" (Hollan).

The operationalisation of the 1983 National Health Policy and 2000 National Population Policy including the RCH and NRHM/NHM strategy has not been taken up with the sincerity and zeal they deserve. The old authoritarian and Neo-Malthusian mindset continues to be pervasive. There are some diehard 'Population Control' exponents among politicians, bureaucrats, demographers and other sections of the elite, who have not reconciled to the paradigm shift, and who feel more comfortable with an authoritarian policy regime of top-down quantitative targetitis, for achieving soft and quick-fix options in implementation. They often deride the Target-Free approach as one, which leads to complete lack of accountability and lack of quick and visible results on ground to be reflected in periodic reports.

Most of the State Government simply linked together pre-existing Family Planning, Child Survival, Safe Motherhood, RTI and STD Services, and Family Planning remained the dominant force in the equation. They have introduced, with full concurrence of the Central Government, 'Expected Levels of Achievement', which are nothing but an euphemism for 'Top-down' contraceptive specific targets. Incentives and disincentives have been re-introduced with a vengeance, and the ambivalence continues unabated. Community based local plans and monitoring are not given due importance. The 'Quality of Care' indicators are, more often than not, observed in breach for the sake of timely achievement of ELA targets. Fundamental reorientation is yet to take deep roots in the minds of programme leaders and service providers. Selective verticalised disease-specific health care approach pursued by WHO, UN agencies, most of the donors and the Government has made a mockery of the Alma Ata concept of Comprehensive Primary Health Care. In fact, the new Health Policy of 2002 was a retrograde one in this direction.

The ambivalence, contradictions, contestations and challenges around Population issue are not peculiar to India.

They persist in different degrees or shades globally in recent years. One can notice a resurgence of the neo-Malthusian and neo-eugenic concerns garbed in new robes in language, research studies and strategies. The myths and misconceptions are coming back through subtle back door strategy to focus on Family Planning. FP 2020 is an example of this phenomenon. Luckily, there is more vigilance and activism of rights-based and gender-sensitive coalitions, who are trying to apply brakes or critique and influence the diehards.

V Concluding Observations: Suggested Way Forward

Reiteration and re-emphasis of the myths and realities around Population problem remains a sustained advocacy and awareness task for the government, demographic-health institutions and civil society. Towards proper fulfilment of this task involving a continuing process of mindset transformation, I would like to suggest the following:

- Modules and curricula content of courses on population in schools, colleges and universities need to be made inter-disciplinary and holistic covering, inter alia, the myths, misconceptions and realities in the appropriate context.
- Courses on Population and Demography to be revisited. Population studies to be re-named as 'Demology' – the knowledge on Population and Development rather than Demography per se. The streams of Economics, Sociology, Social Psychology, Social Anthropology, Public Health, Medical Sciences and Environment disciplines need re-visit to align with the realistic concepts in Demology.
- Intensive training and re-orientation of academia, bureaucracy, legislators and Programme leaders in the Health Sector on the paradigm shift. NIHFW, IIPS, SIHFWS and other training institutions to take a lead.
- Inter-disciplinary research for evidence building needs to be alive to the realities and myths.

- Rights-based and gender sensitive Policy Advocacy to be carried on in a sustained manner at all levels, to keep the grain separated from the chaff. Policy analysis and monitoring studies to be made concurrent to find out inner contradictions and myths and provide a feedback regularly. Competent civil society and research institutions to be jointly involved in this effort. Myths and misconceptions need to be exposed and busted in the full public domain, and the Reality profile need to be updated from time to time with sensitivity, empathy and humanitarianism. Eternal vigilance is required in this respect.
- Population Programme strategy needs to be scrutinised periodically in Central and State Governments through a lense of myths vs. reality by committees with members committed to human rights, gender, reproductive rights and women's health.
- Needs of women and family (specially the poor and marginalised) for better reproductive health and contraceptives to be assessed at regular intervals locally with two-way dialogues, consultations and counselling (with follow-up) rather than one-way top-down imposition of targets and 'take it or leave it' approach by service providers as is the case at present. 'Camp' approach to Sterilisation and IUD, bereft of dignity, safety and 'Quality of Care' must be banned altogether, along with ELA setting. The CNA to form the basis of community-based work-plans in every village/urban ward. 'QOC' indicators to remain the priority of monitoring at community and facility levels, and rewards, recognition and penalties to be structured around these QOC indicators, particularly for Family Planning and Reproductive Health Services. 'Safety and Impact' audits to be instituted in FP, RCH and Primary Health Care.
- Counselling on Gender and Reproductive Rights with male involvement to internalise and bust the myths

of masculinity and patriarchy has to be a priority in Population and Development efforts.

- Priority to be given to comprehensive 'Population Education' as core curriculum of adolescent girls and boys along with peer leaders, parents and teachers, which has to include ARSH, including sexuality, life skills and marriage counselling. Myths and realities around Population issue to be internalised in the process of this education.
- A life-cycle approach to RCH, Women's Health and well being (of both men and women) is called for. Issues of nutrition, post reproductive health and the needs of the elderly need to be tackled if balanced Population Stabilisation becomes a reality in next three or four decades.
- The issue of skewed Sex Ratio at Birth is a serious gender, human rights and development concern in the demographic transition towards population stabilisation. The policies and strategies on Population and Development need to be congruous with each other and be alert towards this disastrous phenomenon. Quick-fix solutions for population control (such as One or Two child norm/incentives and disincentives) are counter-productive and exacerbate adverse sex ratio at birth further as seen in China. The laws impacting on this issue need to be enforced with rigour and zeal.
- Last, but not the least, there has to be paradigm shift in the centralised top-down management style of governance, shorn of real decentralisation, delegation and people's participation. Verticalised disease and theme specific health and contraceptive plans from above is mythical and presumptive, and realism comes only when there is decentralised need-based integrated plans and programmes from the community. The logistics and manpower planning become more realistic. There is synergy, convergence and better acceptability and impact as well as cost-effectiveness. People feel more involved and more knowledgeable of their entitlements,

rights and obligations. Population programmes are better implemented with transparency and accountability at all levels in this management style paradigm. The diversity of needs is taken care of with a high degree of realism. The myths breakdown in the people's minds as also in the minds of Programme Managers and Policy and Strategy leaders. Population problem becomes People's Problem, and Population programme becomes 'People's Programme'.

I would like to end my Oration now by agreeing with Prof. Amartya Sen that 'Cooperation' rather than 'Authoritarianism' in the conceptualisation and tackling of the Population problem is the most effective way forward...

(Copy of the oration delivered on 3 December 2014 at the National Institute of Health and Family Welfare, New Delhi)

Annexure - III

My Tryst with the Law on Pre-birth Sex Selection

The PC-PNDT Act was enacted in 2003. But because of the lackadaisical attitude of the government at the Centre and the states; serious incongruities and contradiction in the policy; and the prevailing 'social mindset' against a female child; sex ratio at birth is declining. Constant vigilance and proactive supervision is the need of the hour.

As the Registrar General and Census Commissioner, in March 1991, when I looked at the fresh results of the1991 census, the phenomenon of adverse sex ratio at birth confronted me. I flagged the issue of sharp decline in sex ratio in the 0-6 age group pointing towards increased sex selective elimination during the previous decade (1981-91). The stark statistics woke the government up, and on being nudged by civil society activists, the Central Government enacted the law known as Pre-natal Diagnostic Techniques (PNDT) Act 1994. But the lobby of vested interests viewed it as a law that was framed not to penalise the erring doctors and ultrasonologists easily. The law came into force in 1996 after much dilly-dallying and was not implemented in spirit.

When I was working as a Secretary in the Ministry of Health and Family Welfare in 2000, the civil society activists led by Dr. Sabu M. George, Centre for Enquiry into Health and Allied Themes (CEHAT) and Mahila Sarvangeen Utkarsh Mandal (MASUM), filed a Public Interest Litigation (PIL) in the Supreme Court. We began to proactively implement the law in the states and districts. Sabu was a great activist, he supported us and also criticised our actions of omissions and commissions. The first two cases of well-planned and well-orchestrated surprise raids with decoy customers in Faridabad district shook the vested interest groups, and the methodical handling of the cases ended in conviction engendered hope across the government and civil society organisations that the law does have teeth and can be implemented if there is a strong will and determination. I played the role of activating the law implementation machinery at state and district levels through regular monitoring, reviews and involvement of activists, civil society and medical professionals in varied ways. The Central Supervisory Board met regularly and training/orientation of appropriate authorities was given a practical shape.

The suggestions for amendments of the law were processed and the amended Act, known as the Pre-conception and Pre-natal Diagnostic Techniques (PC-PNDT) Act 2003, was enacted giving more teeth to the law, and thus widening the scope of sex selection and making it more gender-sensitive. More and more cases got instituted and yet sadly even today, there are still not many substantive cases. A lot more remains to be done. Constant vigilance and proactive supervision is the need of the hour. During my stint with the civil society (after my superannuation from government), we have been having the rendezvous with the issue of adverse sex ratio at birth, which I consider as one of the most dangerous issues facing India. Lack of focus on law implementation including the lackadaisical attitude of the government at the Centre and the states; serious incongruities and contradiction in the policy front (e.g. the restrictive two-child norm exacerbating the practice of sex selection); and the authorities showing helplessness on the plea or alibi of the prevailing 'social mindset' where there is preference for a son and aversion for a daughter; are complicating the issue and worsening the sex ratio at birth all the more. The intersectionality of this phenomenon needs to be recognised and tackled while making law enforcement more accountable and focussed. In no case should the social mindset plea blur the accountability of law enforcement authorities. Targets and timeline accountability should be set for each area and monitored very closely. Surprise raids resorting to decoy customers have to be a frequent phenomenon in medical facilities. The assistance of passionate and honest social activists and community-based organisations need to be taken in this effort. Care must be taken not to resort to gender insensitive monitoring of poor rural women's pregnancies. Instead, medical clinics and diagnostic facilities should be the target of monitoring. This has brought good results in the past too.

We have a good law. Let us not give it a bad name. The motto should be to implement the law in letter and spirit. All that is needed to catch the culprits and punish them, is firm political and administrative "will", generous resources (human and financial) and stern accountability with rewards as well as punishments. Each functionary dealing with the law on sex selection and the policies and programmes around the issue of adverse sex ratio at birth needs to be passionate about her/his work. In short, they need to have a 'tryst' with this issue of saving the girls (*Beti Bachao*).

Annexure - IV

My Power Point Presentation to Ministers and Secretaries on the Eve of the National Beti Bachao Launch

BETI BACHAO

Improving Child Sex Ratio, BBBP
Workshop, Panipat, 20-21 Jan, 2015

- Sex Ratio at Birth
- Child Sex Ratio
- Sex Selection/Determination (Pre-Birth)
- Sex- Selective Abortion
- Prevalence and Spread

- Experience and Promising Initiatives (Since The 1980'S)
- Laws/Policies/Strategies (Govt)
- Civil Societies/Community
- Gaps/Deficiencies/Challenges
- Experience and Promising Initiatives (Since The 1980'S)
- Laws/Policies/Strategies (Govt)
- Civil Societies/Community
- Gaps/Deficiencies/Challenges
- Use Decoys/Surprise Raids/Technology
- Rational Use of Ultrasound
- Rewards/Recognition/Penalties-for/Against Exemplary Detection, Prosecution, vis-a-vis Negligence,

Inaction, Complicity

- Special Drives/Campaigns/Trials
- Targeted Time-Bound Strategies/Action Plans (Quarterly)
- Effective Mechanisms of Planning, Monitoring and Evaluation
- Community-Based Accountability Framework (at Each Ward/Mohalla/Village)
- Target Each Clinical/Diagnostic Facility
- Employ Innovative Intrusive Audits
- Participation of Pro-Active Vigilante Community Groups
- Supervisory Boards Strengthened
- Imaginative Schemes of Incentives for Births of Girl Child
- Safety of Girl Child Ensured/Zero Tolerance
- Gender Sensitization
- Innovative Advocacy/Communication Strategies
- Each M.P/MLA/Pri-Ulb Member in High-Focused 'Beti Bachao' States/Districts to take Responsibility
- Stop The Demographic Disaster At Any Cost
- Sooner, The Better

Annexure - V

My First Solo Pilgrimage to Shirdi

My trips to Shirdi since 1995 have invariably been with friends, family or a group of devotees. The first trip I undertook to Shirdi alone was in December, 2002. This was a unique experience for me with Sai Baba in His abode.

In October, 2002, I got an invitation to speak at an international conference being organized at Loni near Ahmednagar in Maharashtra. Immediately, I thought of a Shirdi trip from there after attending the conference. Then, I was told by the conference organisers that they are putting me up at Garodia Hotel at Shirdi as Loni is not far from Shirdi and there is scarcity of accommodation there. I was overjoyed and thought that Baba is arranging my stay at Shirdi, as I could spend more time with Him. I was wistfully looking forward to my visit.

Shri C. B. Satpathyji had sent me two books for review for publication in the 2003 New Year issue of the 'Sai Heritage', namely,

(1) "Sai the Master" by Sri E. Bhardwaj, and

(2) "Life of Sai Baba" (a composite volume) by Shri B.V. Narasimhaswami published in October, 2002. I read both the books and started writing the reviews from 1 December 2002. When Satpathyji asked me on 3rd December to send the reviews by the weekend, I told him that I have finished one

review and the other one could be completed after my return from Shirdi, where I am going on 4th December. He conveyed his obeisance to Baba through me.

However, I completed the review of the other book on 3rd December night and sent the manuscripts before I left for Delhi airport on 4th December at 11.45 a.m. The reading of these two books surcharged my mind with Baba's leelas and prepared me emotionally to meet Him in His place of rest alone for next few days. My flight to Aurangabad via Mumbai reached by 5 p.m. I took the journey by road from Aurangabad to Shirdi by a taxi. The sunset had painted the western sky with orange hue. I was looking forward to see Baba in His abode wistfully, while doing evening Arati mentally. Near Kopergaon, the taxi driver took me to a "Sai Dham" built by a devotee, who knew Satpathyji. It appeared as if he was awaiting my arrival. He showed me the meditation hall with a huge painting of Baba, the main temple with a big statue of Baba and another room with photos and painting of Baba and Satpathyji. It was as if Sai Baba arranged for this reception and my darshan, before I reached Shirdi.

When I reached Shirdi, I participated in Shej Arati standing outside the side window of Samadhi Mandir, where I could have the darshan of Baba. After Arati, I went to Gurusthan and to Dwarkamayee. I sat at Dwarkamayee for some time and came to the hotel around midnight. I was undecided in my mind about getting up around 3.30 a.m. next morning for Kakad Arati, and requested for a wake-up call at 6 a.m.

Exactly at 3.40 a.m., I got up, as if someone had come to wake me up. Was it Baba's call through the humming of mosquitoes? I felt the urge to get ready for going to the Mandir for attending Kakad Arati and Abhishek. I quickly took bath and rushed barefoot. I took the long winded queue, which was moving slowly. I had, however, no sense of impatience, restlessness, anger or despondency. No sense of helplessness or ego; rather a thrill of expectation 'Shraddha' and 'Saburi'. I went back to my childhood and early rustic life of adolescence, when there was a sense of normalcy and ordinary living; mingling with the 'aam adami' joys. That was pre-IAS, no VIP out-of-turn treat – more normal and matter-of-fact (swabhav). Baba gave me back this! The group souls – all wistfully looking forward to Baba's darshan and only Baba for grace, help and favour. Only looking to Him – the Samarth Sadguru and Sathi Akhirka.... I moved very slowly hall after hall. But there were many ahead of me, who were perhaps waiting since midnight or so. What devotion, what steadfastness, what patience! I bowed down to these souls!

I saw a devotee from Yamunanagar, who is a trustee of Shimla Sai temple behind me. He recognized me and was getting disheartened, when the door to the main hall – the sanctum sanctorum was closed, and the Kakad Arati started at 5 a.m. I gave him solace and sat down on the seat and witnessed the Arati on the close-circuit TV and got immersed in it. Perhaps, Baba had His plan to make me more comfortable at the very early hours of the morning, when I was tired and dozing off and on. I sang the Arati and saw the Abhishek.

A little before 7 a.m., the main hall door opened and I proceeded in the queue to the main hall. I had a grand Darshan of Baba in His Samadhi Mandir. When I stood near the Samadhi, the Chhota Arati and Puja was done. The priest looked at me and smiled. I told him about Satpathyji, and he was very thrilled. I put my head on Baba's Samadhi, and gave three petals of red roses to be put there. The priest gave me three different coloured roses from Baba's Samadhi and charan.

I left the Samadhi Mandir very contented and fulfilled. I felt very light hearted with Baba's grace and compassion, and His unique ways of reflecting your positive sentiment and attitude.

I went again to the Samadhi Mandir around 10 a.m. This time, a trustee of the Sai Sansthan, who recognized me, took me straight to Baba's Samadhi. I put my head on Baba's paduka and stayed near the Samadhi touching it. It was a feeling of exhilaration touching Baba's Samadhi, where Baba has been lying for the last 90 years. After getting Prasad and flowers, I left for Loni for attending the Rural Health Conference.

I came back to Shirdi by 7 p.m., and visited Nanda Deep, Lendi garden and Dwarkamayee. I saw the Palanquin procession. I participated in the Shej Arati very close at range. It was a very thrilling experience indeed! Baba's eyes and face were very expressive, shining and exuding compassion and grace! It was a meditative, sweet and smiling expression of my Sadguru! After Arati, I got very close to Baba's Samadhi again, waved my hand before the Diya, got Prasad, and came back to the place of stay with fullness of Anand. I penned a short poem before going to bed:

"Baba is great! Oh Sai Baba, You are great. Words fail to express what I feel at your abode of rest – Shirdi! Every moment here with You is an experience to be treasured for eternity: this life and beyond. Time and space, 'Oh Baba!'

This was the first time that I came, stayed and moved in your abode, Baba, all alone. I wished to have such experience with You for some time. Normally, I should feel lonely in such circumstances, as I am used to a social life. I did not. Rather I felt the bliss of silence. No one except You, Baba and this soul: a soul and the Divine Super Soul. I looked at You; You looked at me. I beckoned You; You beckoned me... I looked with wistful eyes, Like a lover to her Beloved.... The silence within speaks and discourses...

How nice, the Divine Leela... You look at me, take care of me Like a Mother to Her child. Oh Sai Maa!"

I started tuning a song that Satpathyji wrote in Oriya:

"Come Sai, come near me.
Let the dust of your feet
trickle into the emptiness
of innermost heart...."

(English translation of the first
stanza of Sai Bhajan in Oriya)

I was again in the temple complex next morning. Again, I was straight in front of Baba and His resting place. I prostrated on the floor close to His Samadhi and did not feel like getting up. I was crying. It was an empty hall, prior to the Noon Arati. I was allowed to stand on the right side of Baba in the front row with my back on the pillar. I went into 'Dhyan' until Noon Arati started. When I opened my eyes, I could see Baba's eyes and face were opening up, with an expression of smile and approval. I felt for a minute as if He is alive!

I sang Arati in full throat in unison with the lead singer. After all, I was the child crying before the Mother! I had a wishful thought that Baba in His Samadhi is listening! That there is a luminous blue light around His bones (body). As we (all the devoted souls in a group) address Him with a sense of concentration and purity of feeling from the innermost depth of our hearts, He is responding with a positive divine aura and emitting soothing feeling of joy (Sat-chit-anand) all round! The sense of satisfaction of the souls as they evolve in this process is much higher and more sustained in quality and depth than any other satisfaction one gets in this mundane world. Baba gives it plentifully!

After the Arati, I paid obeisance before the paduka and Samadhi for a while. I was taken to the rear reception room by the Sansthan Executive Officer, who happened to be there to receive the Health Minister of Andhra Pradesh. I was given the honour of gift of a woollen shawl worn by Baba, 2003 Diary and Baba's garland. I took leave of Baba with a heavy heart and left Shirdi. Throughout the return journey (road journey from Shirdi to Aurangabad and air journey to Delhi) my mind was surcharged with 'Sai mood' – the madness that Sai gives you, if you go near Him alone. Nothing else matters!

Annexure - VI

What it Feels Like to be in Sai Consciousness

(Excerpts from my book *The Eternal Sai Consciousness*, Sterling Publishers, New Delhi, 2015)

Being Part of Sai Consciousness

A few suggestions:

- Pursue Bhakti intensely, leading to 'Samarpan' bhava. Satsang, Bhajan and Selfless service. Understand the subtlety of the nine types of Devotion (Navdabhakti).
- Cultivate firm Faith (Shraddha) and devotional love, with Patience, Perseverance and Courage (Saburi) for Sadguru and God.
- Resort to humility, conscientious discrimination (Vivek), dispassion (Vairagya), forgiveness, compassion, piety, contentment and equanimity in joyful or sorrowful situations.
- Attitude of 'Fakiri'—magnanimity, universalism, generosity and bliss.
- Compassionate service to the distressed and needy (human beings, animals, plants and inanimate Nature).
- Swaddhyay (Reading and self-introspection), Shravan (Hearing), and Manan (Contemplation) of literature on

Devotion and Spiritualism. Assimilate all that you read or hear and discover the essence of messages. Regular reading of *Shri Sai Satcharita* is very useful.

- Try to put the messages in your conduct and day-to-day life.
- Rational and balanced management of time, thoughts, speech, action and environment, which will be conducive to cultivation of Sai Consciousness.
- Regularity in and gradual intensification of Meditation and Guru Sadhana for fixity of mind and chitta. The universalizing potential of "Budhiyoga" in modern life of hyper activities is tremendous.
- Minimise worldly material needs and pursuits, while not neglecting your legitimate responsibilities. Be temperate in eating and other sense satiations.
- Ethical conduct and good life. Cultivate mostly sattwik qualities, less resort to Rajasik and the least resort to Tamasic qualities in thought and action.
- Tolerance and appreciation of all religions, sects or paths, and respect for all Sadgurus Saints and Perfect Masters.
- Having a positive outlook towards life's travails and keeping away from negativities about you and others.
- Right perspective and clarity on 'Maya', cosmology, Brahm Vidya, Guru's role, Sagun and Nirgun worship, Karmaphal Prarabhda, and Nishkam Karma—all inherent in Sai Consciousness. The empirical human consciousness steeped in Ignorance (Avidya) is transformed into higher Consciousness.
- No pomp or show or ritualism in Bhakti Marg, Guru Sadhana or prayers. 'Interiorize' 'religion, as Guru Nanak used to say.
- Stay away from vices, jealousy, greed, avarice, lust, anger, pride, hatred, ego (including spiritual ego), violence, gossips, hankering after worldly fame, honour or

recognition, falsity, cheating, bad company or association and useless arguments or debates.

- Non-reliance on or exhibition of miracles or other psychic power (Siddhis). Any miracle happening in your life be treated as the Grace of Sadguru and God.
- Try to achieve 'Purushartha', which implies the four fruits of life, namely:
  - **Dharma (**Conscientious and righteous discharging of imperative duty)
  - **Artha (**Right livelihood and honest earning)
  - **Kama (**Satisfaction of legitimate desires) and
  - **Moksh** (Liberation from limitations of conditioned life of materialism, leading to spiritual bliss).

  There are four types of spiritual emancipation. You have the potential to achieve any of these:

  - Salakya (attaining the same region of consciousness as God or Sadguru)
  - Sarupya (attaining the same image as Sadguru or God)
  - Sampiya (experiencing the Bliss of being extremely dear to God or Sadguru); and
  - Sayujya (experiencing total spiritual emancipation)

  Bhakti yoga is the best path towards 'Moksh' (emancipation). One can develop a life of devotional 'mysticism', which implies a "gradual ascent in the scale of spiritual values, experience and spiritual ideals." As such, it will be many sided in its development and "as rich and complete as life itself."

- Please find the essence of Sai Consciousness in prayers of different religions. An example of a Christian prayer is given here:

"Lord! Make me an instrument of your peace.
Where there is hatred, let me sow Love.
Where there is injury, Pardon;
Where there is doubt, Faith;
Where there is despair, Hope;
Where there is darkness, Light;
And where there is sadness, Joy.
O Divine Master!
Grant that I may not so much seek
To be consoled as to console;
To be understood as to understand;
To be loved as to love
For it is in giving that we receive.
It is in pardoning that we are pardoned,
And it is in dying that We are born to Eternal life...."

(St. Francis of Assissi)

Being part of Sai Consciousness in a sustained manner tantamounts to eternal pure God Consciousness ultimately—the state of Eternal Truth, Existence, Consciousness and Bliss (Sat Chid Anand).

Index